The Professional

LYNDON B. JOHNSON

Books by
William S. White

The Taft Story

Citadel: The Story
of the U.S. Senate

Majesty and Mischief:
A Mixed Tribute to F.D.R.

The Professional:
Lyndon B. Johnson

The Professional

LYNDON B. JOHNSON

WILLIAM S. WHITE

HOUGHTON MIFFLIN COMPANY BOSTON
THE RIVERSIDE PRESS CAMBRIDGE

THIRD PRINTING   C

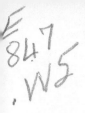
Again: To Cia and Victoria White

CONTENTS

1

TRAGIC FLIGHT

I T WAS A LONG, LONG ROAD THAT HAD led, by accident and by tragedy, to the office which he had candidly sought and in honorably tough combat had lost to another. For almost three years, Lyndon B. Johnson had loyally served as Second Man to the First Man in the United States, John F. Kennedy.

Sometimes it had been a quizzical loyalty. Sometimes it had been an anxious loyalty as he saw (here and there) what he believed to be mistakes which he could not correct and which he would not mention to the man who, though a decade younger, was nevertheless the chief to whom he had pledged, and given, the best help that was in him. There had been friendship, too; a wry, ripening, adult friendship based mainly on mutual respect and mutual knowledge of a happily shared competence in their art between two of the most gifted professional politicians of this century.

On a bright November day in Dallas, Texas, the thin, bitter yelp of rifle shots had just closed the life of John Fitzgerald Kennedy of Massachusetts, the thirty-fifth President of the United States. Now, in an airplane already warming up to return to Washington with the dead body of a President and with the quick and troubled person of his successor, Lyndon Baines Johnson of Texas, his head slightly lowered and forward, and his shoulders already hunched under the new, great burdens, swore faithfully to serve as the thirty-sixth president of the United States. The old words of the oath were repeated by the new President with, again and again, a breaking sigh.

As he stood in the aircraft parked on the slick, dirty asphalt of that most curiously unhuman, curiously forsaken thing in all the world, an airstrip in the gathering dark, he thought first of all of the man who had fallen. And behind heavy eyeglasses glistening under the hurriedly devised lamps set up to photograph this aching moment in history, Johnson wept for Kennedy the chief, but also for Kennedy the companion. In the old days in the United States Senate when Johnson was First Man as majority leader, and John Kennedy Second Man as a junior senator, he had been "ol' Jack." But from election night in 1960, he had been to Lyndon Johnson only "Mr. President," or "The President."

These were real tears of grief deeply felt. The notion that the strong and tough—and strong and tough Lyndon Johnson has always been—do not really cry is an absurdity, in public life as in all other life. Winston Churchill, the very arch-type of the indomitable, could shed tears when the strains of "Land of Hope and Glory" swept out over the evening air from a military band in Hyde Park. True politicians, with very rare exceptions, are men of sentiment though seldom of sentimentality; their working materials are men and women and human emotions and memories and traditions, quite as much as abstract and impersonal problems. The latter things perforce they tolerate and wrestle with; the former are welcome, in their blood and bones.

Sometimes, in the past, Kennedy and Johnson had joked together about that "single heart-beat," so long and so well beloved of the more tired forms of journalism, which alone separated the winner at the Los Angeles Democratic convention of 1960 from the also-ran. They had done this with much of that bantering, half-fond, half-mordant, self-deprecatory wit with which old soldiers sometimes discuss tomorrow's engagement, wondering aloud which of them will survive.

Now the thing over which they had casually laughed had, in incomprehensible horror, become the reality which neither had ever, for a moment, credited in mind or heart. So Johnson wept; not simply for a true friend who had gone, and not simply for a gay and gallant leader whose magnanimity had enabled his erstwhile rival to make of the Vice-Presidency, usually a shadowy and unreal office, a place worthy of a man of skill and purpose.

But the new President's mind, as he stood in the parked aircraft in Dallas, turned from personal grief to fear and concern for the Republic which he had just given his oath to maintain. Lyndon Johnson's intellectual processes have always been, under great stress, almost reflexive, of an instantaneous, tactile sensitivity unique in my experience as an observer of public men.

He felt, all at once, the whole weight of the country in his hands. And he knew with an absolute certainty that he must act at once over the whole range of a dozen problems. He must see not only that the continuity of the Republic was maintained without break, but also that it must *seem* to be so maintained. He had no time for conscious thought.

It was one of many somber ironies that he had also had no time for thought just short of three years before in this very city of Dallas where in fleeting seconds the victory of the Kennedy-Johnson ticket was perhaps assured. He and his wife had taken the Kennedy-Johnson campaign to Dallas. As they entered the Adolphus Hotel a band of extreme rightists jostled and all but physically attacked, not simply the six-foot-three vice-presidential candidate, but also his small, brunet wife who clung to his arm, her determined head coming just below his shoulder.

Instinct told him what reason had no time to say: not simply that he must walk through this hostile crowd in poise and dignity, *but that he must do it very slowly so that this scene would be indelibly impressed upon the people of Texas,* whose shortcomings have never included harassment, by mob or otherwise, of any lady, anytime, anywhere. He walked slowly indeed, so that television and newspaper photographs would tell their undeniable story of one of those forms of extremism which he had fought for thirty years in public life. He wanted the people, first in Texas and then all over the country, to see clearly where—as he had so long warned—extremism could carry a community, a party or a nation.

And the people, certainly in Texas, did see and sense and almost smell it. For from that moment onward a state leaning by every discernible indication to the Nixon-Lodge presidential ticket began to turn, instead, to

Kennedy and Johnson. It was, of course, a big state in electoral terms, one of the most critical in the country. A good many observers, of whom this writer was one, later concluded that the ugly sights and sounds in the lobby of that hotel had made John F. Kennedy President and Lyndon B. Johnson Vice-President of the United States. Much could be said, by the most objective standards, for the validity of that estimate. After all, it was, as it turned out, the closest presidential election in American history. If he never accepted without qualification that reading of how destiny was turned, John Kennedy never rejected it.

"Old Lyndon," he once told me, "sure took his time taking himself and Bird through that lobby—and it wasn't by accident; that instinct of his just told him what to do and how to do it."

At all events, it was this same capacity to function best in disaster that now served Lyndon Johnson. Even as the coffin of the dead President was being made ready for the airplane, again without conscious thought, he perceived the harsh, wholly demanding and wholly unexpected imperative: the first thing that must be done was to put together the threads of a national union that had parted like a broken seam at the moment John Kennedy died in a Dallas hospital.

He did not consciously plan any of this; he does not now even recall in proper chronological sequence exactly what he did: the consoling, as best he could, of Mrs. Kennedy; the orders for an immediate swearing-in of a new President so that the constitutional mandate passed at once to the new head of government; the orders for an immediate take-off to Washington; the calm, decisive instructions to such subordinates as were already about him in Dallas; the orders sent ahead to Washington to other officials who until moments before had been Kennedy officials and Kennedy choices.

As the plane flew northward and eastward to Washington, President Johnson felt the second of his griefs and the third of his agonizing concerns. This most poignant and horribly dramatic assassination since Abraham Lincoln's murder at the close of the Civil War had occurred in a state which had made the new President its foremost son—in sustained power and influence, though not in the drama of folklore, comparable only in its legends to Sam Houston, who freed Texas from Mexico. It had occurred in a state he loved; where he was host. And in those early moments when no one knew the identity of the assassin or the nature of his motives there lay brooding perhaps the gravest threat since the fall of Lincoln to national unity, to national order, to the ideal of one country forever bound together.

For if it should turn out—and at this moment the new President did not know—that some sectional or rightist antagonist of the late President was the figure behind the rifle, the nation would face frightful bitterness and venom, sectional or ideological, and blindly unreasoning.

So he grieved for what had been done by one man to another and what might be done to a decent people in a decent state and section; to the common life of a nation facing vast external perils; to justice, tolerance, compassion, brotherhood, order, peace and rational political dissent, in the oldest practicing democracy in the world.

All of what Lyndon Johnson felt in these moments he

has never fully told to another person, and perhaps never will. Shortly, the cloud was lifted from his native state and its people by the disclosure that the assassination had been done by an itinerant named Lee Harvey Oswald, an admirer of Communist Cuba.

As the aircraft was turned toward Washington, it carried two somber weights. One, Kennedy's coffin, covered by the flag for which both the dead man and the living had fought in the far Pacific. The other—terrible if impalpable, darkly profound if invisible—the Gethsemane of a new President whose task was not only to guide a suddenly stricken country but also to see that the assassin's trail was followed to the end, even if it might bring indictment upon his own people. Johnson also could not know then whether one of his oldest and closest friends, Governor John Connally, would live or die in the Dallas hospital where he lay wounded. He only knew that evil chance had thrown upon him a kind of responsibility never before suffered by a man suddenly made President by the death of another. The very cause to which he had given his political life—a politics of moderation and restraint, a drawing together of sections and factions and interests—might die from the same burst of violence that was sending this presidential airplane on its somber mission.

He feared that a chaos of hatred and counterhatred—ideological, sectional, racial, religious—might now sweep the country. He feared for the union of the states and, in a lesser way, for the union of the Democratic Party. It was to avoid the least possibility of just such cross currents that he had in 1960 at the hot, clamorous Democratic national convention in Los Angeles, astounded so many of his associates and friends by agreeing to accept second place on the Democratic ticket.

Much that is too complicated has been written of the early morning-after of that urgent night at Los Angeles when John F. Kennedy at last defeated Lyndon B. Johnson for the presidential nomination. What really happened was quite simple. Kennedy, recognizing the fact that his nomination had been made possible only by the support of iron-handed urban—and largely Catholic—Democratic leaders from the North and East, told Johnson just about this:

"You have long declared for moderation and mutual tolerance in the party—for a time when there would be 'no North, no South, no East, no West' but one united party and country. If you are not on the ticket with me, that ticket is going to lose, and you know it." Some of Johnson's oldest friends, the late Speaker of the House Sam Rayburn of Texas among them, found it impossible to understand how perhaps the greatest master ever of the most difficult of all political forums, the United States Senate, should now sit lower at the party table than one of the most junior members of that body. These urgently pressed their advice: "Lyndon, don't do it. You can't do it. Just stay on as majority leader of the Senate."

Johnson heard them out; but he did not reflect long. He agreed from that moment onward to use his sword under Kennedy's command. And use it he did, notably and effectively in the South, and most notably and effectively among Protestant groups everywhere which were in fear of Kennedy's religion. It was, as he said in the campaign, a matter of "Austin to Boston." Austin, the capital of Texas, was a great metropolis to Lyndon Johnson as a boy, the shining city-goal to a youngster living on a parched ranch in the dry, dun, live oak- and mesquite-covered hills surrounding the hamlet of Johnson City, which was the post office address of his family.

There was an inevitable outcry from Johnson's supporters, from all over the country but notably from his native South. Many honestly and deeply believed that the abler man had unwisely accepted a subordinate place to a much younger, much less experienced, and much less tried and trustworthy political campaigner and leader. There was harsh and sullen hurt in the South; even mutters that "Lyndon has sold out."

It was said by some, in their disappointment and anger, that no man in modern politics had given up so much for so little. Pieces of the silver of betrayal could be found by frantically illogical men in the transaction by which the Senate majority leader had put a great career in pawn, for the iffy honor of accompanying a Catholic presidential nominee toward a strongly possible November defeat.

Johnson has a strong streak of realism—a realism sometimes gustily contemptuous not of honest, naked ignorance, but of the deliberate inability of precious or pretentious men to see a fact for a fact. Now it was blended with an equally strong sense of compassion for those excessively loyal ones whose concern for his future both annoyed and touched him. He had made an undoubted personal sacrifice. But, because of the sharp, edgy sense of private reticence that lies deep in him, he did not like it at all when others yammered as though a rationally generous act on his part was actually some oriental self-immolation. Impatient though he was, he could, however, understand the sentiments, if not the lack of cold good sense, of those who were criticizing his submission to Kennedy as a surrender of the South.

Back in Washington after the convention, he had dictated a masterly form letter which put the position as clearly as he knew how to put it:

Dear Friend:

You are a little bit disappointed at the way the convention turned out, and so, I think was everyone. For no man can go into a political convention and come out with everything he wants. For my own part, I feel strongly that no man ever fulfills an obligation by turning his back on a duty to which he is called. I neither sought nor solicited the vice-presidency, but when the invitation to join Senator Kennedy on the ticket came, I had the choice of turning tail and abandoning any opportunity for Texas and the South to have a voice in the carrying out of national policy or of repaying the confidence of the Democrats from all over the country who voted for me for President.

You have been a real friend, and it would be my strong hope that by the time this campaign is over, you can give the Democratic ticket the same confidence and support you so generously gave to me.

Now, the new President of the United States who had, indeed, sacrificed much for moderation and unity within his party, had reason to fear it might be destroyed along with the man he had truly and honorably served.

Long before this, and indeed all through his career, the new President had known, perhaps more than any other public man, the pains and danger of clinging to the middle

way. For years, first as a congressman and then as a senator, he had been regarded by many in Texas—always a
perilous many for his comfort—as far too liberal. Sometimes, to them, he was almost a "Socialist" or "Communist." For years in other parts of the nation, notably in
the liberal and urban East, he had meanwhile been denounced as a southern Tory and Bourbon. For years he
had fought off these opposite pressures, seeing them as
senseless clichés used by people with a passion for labeling
things and an unbelievable incapacity to understand that
in American politics there is not always pristine, simon-
pure right and simon-pure, pristine wrong, with no decent
ground between.

This sort of oversimplification he had long borne, in his
former offices, simply going on doggedly with a politics of
reason, of rational compromise, trying for what is indispensable in a free, democratic society: an informed and
reasonable consensus in a government which must, precisely, rest upon the consent of the governed. Now as
President of the United States, he was in a quite different
job, the job of ultimate responsibility over all. Would moderation, reason and political tolerance now prevail in this
frightened, saddened, momentarily almost hysterical
country, as the story of the assassination of a truly beloved
President unfolded?

It would if Lyndon Johnson could bring it about. And
to this highest of all his immediate objectives he was resolved to bring all the resources of one of the most formidable political minds of our time—a mind so regarded by
those most perceptive and coldly objective of all judges,
the professional politicians in both parties. And he would

put into play that intangible quality of talent which never can be created, no matter how long and sustained the effort. If ever a man was born with the political gift, as a great violinist is born to the violin, that man is Lyndon Johnson. The man now lying dead in the aircraft was one of the many witnesses to this fact; John F. Kennedy himself had told friends before the 1960 convention that no other aspirant for the Presidency had Johnson's inherent capacity.

So, with a binding up of the nation's wounds his first great aim, and with a conscious, grateful adoption of that phrase and purpose from the Lincoln tragedy of a century before, the thirty-sixth President opened, as the aircraft approached Washington, perhaps the most urgent series of actions ever taken by a chief executive in time of peace. Deeply troubled for Mrs. Kennedy, with whom his relationship from the 1960 campaign forward had been one of easy and often humorously underplayed liking on both sides, he thought first of what he might do to make the days immediately ahead no more frightful for her than they must be.

First, he considered the arrangements for official mourning which were to make of Washington, on the three days to come, a city of somberness far darker, far more piercing, somehow, to the human heart than even the period of mourning for the new President's great friend and mentor, Franklin D. Roosevelt.

Meantime, as the jet streams swept by the plane window, he wrote out his first statement as President to the people of the United States, which he would read when the aircraft landed in the dank darkness at Andrews Air Force Base near Washington.

"This is a sad time for all people. We have suffered a loss that cannot be weighed. For me, it is a deep, personal tragedy. I know that the world shares the sorrow that Mrs. Kennedy and her family bear. I will do my best. That is all I can do. I ask your help, and God's."

2

CRISIS
OF TRANSFER

HIS BEST, THEN, HE BEGAN TO DO.
The White House, naturally, was to remain Mrs. Kennedy's until she could make her arrangements for moving. Johnson himself, his wife, and their younger daughter, Lucy Baines, would continue to live for those days in the Norman house in northwest Washington that they had bought three years before. Their elder daughter, Lynda Bird, was away, a student at the University of Texas. The house, called "The Elms," had been more than adequate for the Johnsons while he was still Vice-President. It had sheltered, besides the family, half a dozen Negro servants who always moved with the assurance of long and affectionate familiarity with their employers; among those truly close to her whom Mrs. Johnson was shortly to take to the Capitol to hear the new President's first address to Congress was the old family cook, Mrs. Zephyr Wright.

But now The Elms was caught in a madness for which, spacious and roomy as it was, it had never been designed. More Secret Service men now piled in to take up residence inside the house and to patrol outside, joining their veteran colleagues who had long been on rather relaxed duty there when its resident was only a Vice-President who had

often barked in exasperation at them, while they smiled
with slow tolerance. He had felt himself altogether too
guarded even then; he was shortly to be in a state of re-
signed impatience and amazement at how restricted his
movements became when the Secret Service first team
moved to The Elms to join the old second team.

Communications became an immediate and imperative
problem. Beforehand, The Elms had only ordinary tele-
phones (except for one, in a security-cloaked place, on
which President Kennedy could reach Vice-President
Johnson directly on a moment's notice) and the Johnsons,
particularly Mrs. Johnson, had often answered the bell
themselves. Now, while great floodlights played everywhere outside and a knot of hard, quiet men flanked the
approaches to the house and stood here and there in the
shrubbery about it, elaborate telephone and radio apparatus was thrust into The Elms with even greater speed, as
one recalls it, than communications equipment was set up
in a command post during the war.

President Johnson established his principal operating
headquarters in a sort of sun room just off a stone patio
which, surrounded by shrubs and flowers, ambles down
toward an undeniably glamorous, heated, outdoor swimming pool. Wherever he has been, Johnson has always,
when he had the money, lived to the hilt; he is neither hostile to, nor ashamed of, wealth nor the least bit interested
in its total absence among associates or friends. If he has
it, it is there to spend, and he spends it. But the Republic
is niggardly with Vice-Presidents in the matter of expense
money. By coincidence, he had only a few weeks before
remarked to a friend: "One sad thing about this job of

mine, ol' fellow; it costs me plenty." He had been spending his own money—or perhaps more exactly, mostly Mrs.
Johnson's money—at the rate of $100,000 a year. Most of
it went for official entertainment; much of it went just to
maintain The Elms. Again, an instance of perhaps excessive thrift in this democracy is its unwillingness to provide
the vice-president with an official residence.

Take the night of Saturday, November 23. Here was the
new President of the United States operating a shaken,
saddened country by telephone from the sun room of a
Norman house in a rather prosperous suburb much like
others which could be found anywhere in this land where
well-off people foregather to live the good life as they see
it.

By dinner-time of this night, Johnson had been President
for some twenty-four hours. And by this time he had,
since returning from Dallas, seen to Mrs. Kennedy's comfort as best he could, rallied his own old staff and the
Kennedy staff, received major intelligence briefings from
military and diplomatic officials. He had also called home
urgently Henry Cabot Lodge, the American Ambassador
to South Viet Nam, to make it very plain that he would
tolerate no more of the backbiting between our embassy
and military officers out there which had troubled Kennedy's last days and impeded military resistance to the
Communist invaders from the North. These and many
other things had been done.

The new President had already talked to most of the
Kennedy Cabinet officers, making it clear that he would
not accept the resignations which protocol and precedent
demanded that they offer. He had already taken the de-

cision, on the way back from Dallas, that the Kennedy team would be kept intact if he could keep it intact. He had told them that they must not even go through the motions of offering to quit. He had also said to all of them that he understood and shared their pain and grief, but that the United States must go on and that he relied upon them all to help him to keep it going on, without a moment's break in time or momentum.

He had already made his decision to retain, if he could, not merely the Kennedy Cabinet—notably including the late President's brother, Attorney-General Robert F. Kennedy, now dazed with sorrow and loss—but also the so-called Palace Guard of academic intellectuals and tough young Irish politicians, which had surrounded Kennedy Some of these had been by no means Johnson admirers at the beginning of the Kennedy administration. Some of them had even been the presumed sources of those stories that Kennedy and Johnson had "broken" or were about to "break" which for nearly three years had made the Vice-President's life a hard one.

There never had been any substance to these rumors. John F. Kennedy from first to last remained loyal to Johnson and Johnson to him. As a Washington journalist with a close and unbroken contact with Johnson and with a satisfactory if necessarily less intimate contact with Kennedy, I knew that both men were repeatedly troubled and embarrassed by stories that Kennedy would "dump" Johnson at the next convention or that Johnson was on the "outs" with Kennedy for this or that reason.

Indeed, Kennedy had told me about a week before his inauguration in January of 1961: "Anybody in this administration who thinks he will promote himself with me by biting at Lyndon Johnson has a very large hole in his head." His manner made it abundantly evident that he wanted this word widely spread. He and Johnson both knew from the very outset that the greatest danger to the success of the administration would be the fomenting of spurious feuds between them which could only result in disorder and weakness.

Actually, the Kennedy-Johnson relationship at the start had been one of mutual respect but of no great proclamations of mutual love: neither man was made of sugar candy and neither man was ever a hypocrite. They knew, surely better than all others, that they had indeed fought a hard and acute—if never a nasty or little—fight for the presidential nomination. They left the Los Angeles convention completely allied in purpose—as, say, the United States and Britain are usually completely allied in purpose—but there were some undeniable bruises from their convention collision and neither was silly enough to deny it to himself or the other.

But as the campaign went forward and Johnson hurled himself into it with a single-minded determination that Kennedy, with his essentially less urgent personality, could envy and appreciate, the bruises began to heal and what had been a Kennedy-Johnson alliance of high effectiveness became also a Kennedy-Johnson alliance of cordial friendship. The impression one gained at the time was that such personal reserve as Kennedy had initially felt was forever melted by two of Johnson's most daring, and most productive, campaign actions.

The first of these was his whistle-stop sortie by train into the South—the area of which Kennedy was most afraid in electoral terms—in which Lyndon Johnson, accompanied all the way by Mrs. Johnson, pleaded for, argued for, and flatly demanded the allegiance of the South to the Kennedy-Johnson ticket. As the jaunty strains of "The Yellow Rose of Texas" endlessly poured out from the campaign train, Johnson appealed not merely to the crowds that came out; he also saw hundreds of local, district and state politicians in private. From them he held many promissory notes; for as Senate majority leader he had done more for the modern South and for modern southern politicians than any other man. He called in his loans, telling the debtors in substance: "It is the Democratic Party—the party of your fathers and grandfathers—that needs you now. And if it comes to that I, Lyndon Johnson, personally need you now. I am calling in my notes; I am calling in my loans. You can't let me down; you can't let Jack Kennedy down."

This thrust from Washington down to the sea at New Orleans was not only the decisive factor in saving the bulk of the South for the ticket; it also stirred élan throughout the presidential candidate's efforts all over the nation. This John Kennedy deeply and especially appreciated. As a member of the Senate he had in fact been closest of all, in human terms and even to a degree in political terms, to southern senators, whose skill and personal honor he deeply valued. It was an odd thing, this special affection of the Massachusetts man for both the South and southerners. He never wanted to part with the South; and when, later, he had to part with some of it over the issue of civil rights, he was saddened more by this than by any other decision he made.

Thus, when Johnson went to the front for him in the South so strongly and so ably—and with disregard for the fact that his own bridges were seemingly being burned all over the region by his loyalty to a Yankee Catholic—Kennedy was never to forget what had been done.

Similarly, he felt a special gratitude to Johnson, a member of the Christian Church, for the most vital thrust of all to neutralize the Catholic issue. This was a televised meeting arranged by Johnson between a group of Houston Protestant ministers and Kennedy, in which the presidential candidate and his ministerial audience frankly exchanged their views in an unprecedented airing of religious differences which proved that these differences could make no honest man less or more an American.

This meeting was widely televised in other quarters of the country at Johnson's suggestion. More than anything else, it broke the back of religious prejudice as a campaign issue. It was an enormous contribution not only to decently effective politics but to national unity.

By the time Kennedy and Johnson took their oaths of office, the thing had progressed to the most genuinely close relationship in history between a President and Vice-President. Kennedy knew this, and Johnson knew it. Both also knew, however, that leaders in war forgive each other more quickly than do followers; both knew that some Kennedy subordinates had not exculpated Johnson from the crime of having opposed "the Boss" at any time at all. Some of the men closest to Kennedy on his personal staff, as distinguished from his Cabinet, felt resentments against

"LBJ" which were so keen—and from their own somewhat limited point of view so real and "loyal"—that they
found it hard to forgive the Texan for being a member of
the team at all.

Of course this irked him humanly. He understood and
valued loyalty and he held no grudge though he often
wistfully wished that those close to Kennedy could understand how the Boss himself felt about LBJ. The situation
annoyed Kennedy, too, though he never in fact knew the
full extent of it. Johnson would have found it unthinkable
to complain to Kennedy about the small slights which, for
a time, were part of his burden. Whatever Johnson's faults,
there is nothing little in him. Even his shortcomings—a
furious impatience at times with slow minds and small motives—what he calls nit-picking and backbiting—are large
and almost excessively candid.

Moreover, he, too, had his too "loyal" followers; the people who could not forgive *Kennedy* the crime of having
opposed *Johnson* at any time at all. But most important
of all, the new President respected the capacity and devotion and undoubted patriotism of the old Kennedy Palace
Guard staff men. He wanted to keep them around not
simply to maintain continuity, he wanted them also because he knew them to be bright and able. All his life he
has respected ability and candid loyalty more than any
other human qualities short of courage and honor.
Whenever in all his career he has faced an extraordinarily
difficult problem he has gone for advice to the man he believes to know most about the matter. It is irrelevant to
him if this happens also to be a man he does not like or
who does not like him.

Lyndon Johnson can make almost anybody like him in the end anyhow, if he works at it, as was shortly demonstrated among the Palace Guard to whom he had appealed to stay on. Though authentically "tough" outside, and as utterly demanding of those around him as he is of himself, he is extraordinarily sensitive and perceptive, especially in personal relationships. It was not simply because his views were "right" that as majority leader of the Senate he was able a dozen times to make conservative lions and liberal lambs lie down together. He did it most of all through the power of personal persuasion, based upon an instinctive, sensitive awareness of the inner feelings—convictions, prejudices, emotions, sticking points—of any man with whom he treats face to face.

As a very young minority leader when the late Senator Robert A. Taft was majority leader of the Senate in 1953, Johnson was the only man in either party who could easily deal with the formidably correct Taft on a perfectly relaxed, unconsciously slightly impudent, even jocular footing. "Bob, Bob!" he might gleefully whisper across the aisle while Taft was inwardly burning at some show of ineptitude by one of his own partisan troops on the Senate floor, "I know you must be very proud of your party today. How are you ever able to find such great minds as that?" Taft would never have tolerated such an observation from even the most senior of his own party associates. But with Johnson he would only smile—an amazing smile compounded of ruefulness, discomfort, outraged decorum, amusement and affection—slightly avert his face and whisper back: "Now, now, Lyndon."

Johnson's decision on his gloomy first Saturday night of

his Presidency to keep personal associates of Mr. Kennedy for his own, subject only to their being willing to stay and help, was, for him, the inevitable one.

With the Kennedy Cabinet, there had been no problem at all. The new President had served with them all, observed them all, agreed and differed with them all, throughout the time he had sat in the Cabinet with Kennedy at its head. He knew them all, sometimes perhaps even better than Kennedy, because of his peculiar gift of empathy.

Long since, he had formed a special admiration for two of them, Secretary of State Dean Rusk and Secretary of Defense Robert McNamara. Of Rusk he had said privately, hardly a month before the assassination of Kennedy, that he was "a good man, a prudent man, a man making no show but always knowing what he is doing and why he is doing it." Indeed, again privately—for as Vice-President he had leaned over backward never to seem to speak in any way for the administration unless asked by the President to do so—he had hotly defended Rusk when, in the aftermath of the Cuban crisis in the autumn of 1962, a magazine article spoke slurringly of the Secretary's contributions to the decision to clear Soviet missiles from Cuba or to go to war. It was made to appear in the article that Rusk had been timid and hesitant; to Johnson this was ugly nonsense. What Rusk had done, as Johnson saw it, was rightly to reserve his judgment, as the senior Cabinet officer, until all sides had been heard. This seemed to Johnson not only the right course, but the obligatory one from where Rusk sat.

LBJ was also sympathetic at the time to United Nations

Ambassador Adlai Stevenson, who had been badly cut up in the article as perhaps an "appeaser." Again, Johnson saw Stevenson's proper role as frankly to present his side of the problem—that is, all the diplomatic implications and all the undoubted objections that would be voiced by many members of the UN. Johnson, although himself a really "tough liner" in the great, grave conference, was not willing to stigmatize others who either held a different view or simply thought it their duty to present one for common inspection.

As to Secretary McNamara, Johnson had made up his mind about him in the very first Kennedy Cabinet meeting in January of 1961. Returning to his office in the Capitol from that meeting, he remarked to a friend: "A man in this new Cabinet to tie to is that young fellow McNamara. I saw him in action for the first time this morning but I think I know what I am talking about. He knew what ought to be done in his department. It was bang, bang, bang. If I were president I would put in my stack with him." When a poker player has absolute confidence in his hand he shoves into the pot his entire stack of chips.

At all events, it was Rusk and McNamara upon whom most of all the new President leaned that Saturday night as the load of a hundred responsibilities fell on his heavy, black-clad shoulders. A few friends were about him in the sun room—one of them the slight, quiet Abe Fortas, who as Undersecretary of the Interior had been a Johnson companion and adviser since the Roosevelt New Deal days of thirty years before.

It was no accident that only Fortas and two or three others were there that night; President Johnson in facing crisis turns first to those with whom, as he says, he has been "often to the bridge and back" meaning roughly those who in danger and possible disaster would never retreat.

Everyone in the sun room, except the new President, was quiet through nearly the whole of that evening. Johnson himself was never so. Sitting at the telephone, he pressed one after the other of its six buttons, calling a lesser official or a Cabinet officer, with no distinction of protocol in his mind. For each there was a brisk, clipped, hurried but calm instruction: "Do this tonight, do this tomorrow, get into touch with so and so."

He was not merely issuing directives, nor was the issuance of directives his sole motive. He was deliberately giving all the key officers of the government all they could possibly do, just as he was burdening himself. He knew their grief, and himself felt it, as occasionally he passed his hand over his forehead, in a half-violent gesture. But he knew they must overcome grief at once, become lost in the immediately necessary things that must be done throughout the government. So he never spoke of grief. He was pulling them all together emotionally and personally, as well as officially. Racing against fear and possible chaos, he dared not let momentum halt or falter.

Amidst it all, he telephoned the Department of Justice and directed J. Edgar Hoover to open at once a full, unsparing inquiry into the assassination in Dallas. He wanted the country to know that no verdict of the Dallas authorities—although he had no question of their integrity of purpose—would be enough. There must be objective, national investigation over which his own state would have no control, no conceivable power to whitewash anybody or any movement or section. He had had, at this point, no time to put in train his second step soon to be taken. This was to be the appointment of a high presidential commission, headed by Chief Justice Earl Warren and dominated by Republican members. His whole motive, which he mentioned to no one that night, letting his actions speak for him, was to establish exactly what had happened in Dallas and by whom it had been done. He felt he owed an aseptic, pitiless, inquiry of justice to the nation and to history.

Meanwhile, however, this inwardly harassed and outwardly rock-like man was aware that the most absolute need for the country's continued safety was to start and sustain a furious, outward-looking and onward-looking presidential activity. The need was to demonstrate, both here and abroad, that the *institution* of the Presidency had not died and could never die.

The contrast between the opening hours and days of the new administration and the opening hours and days of the last previous administration to be installed upon the heels of death—that of Harry S. Truman—could not have been wider. Truman had come to office in almost total ignorance of what Roosevelt had been doing and planning and promising. Indeed, it was an ignorance so profound that the new President entering the White House on an April night in 1945 did not even know that a thing called an atomic bomb had been built.

Truman had hardly been informed by Roosevelt at all. Johnson had not only been kept fully informed by Kennedy, he had been a working, intimate part of all that his chief had done and planned and promised. Thus his capacity, in the academic sense, to undertake the Presidency at a moment's notice had never been in doubt. Through his personal qualities he now had to show that the practical ability to fulfill this capacity was not lacking. There started that first Saturday night two weeks of decision and action from a man who usually now slept no more than four or five hours out of the twenty-four. He was seeing men and women in his office at the rate of ninety a week, seeking more kinds of advice from more kinds of people than any President before had ever done. Sometimes, in this period, he conferred with one or more callers in his limousine on the way from The Elms, where he was spending his brief nights, to the White House, where he was spending his very long days.

A tornado or a cyclone—these were the terms used by some observers. What was not generally known was that Johnson was acting simply as Johnson. He had always believed, in every office he had held, that the greatest enemy of sound public policy is the loss among its leaders of the irreplaceable élan of momentum—a decisive élan in his view that comes when initiative is not only held, but clearly and demonstrably held. Always there has been a controlled hurricane about him; this is his standard operating procedure.

But the President retains an essential inner calm in the middle of the storm, though his outer self may and does shout and demand speed and decision from all those about him. Through these memorable days—fourteen days actually more dramatic in some ways than the storied first hundred days of Franklin Roosevelt—he turned from the large to the small, from the fate of the West to the fate of individual men—to reassure and to help.

His sympathy for the White House staff was both sensitive and active; he knew that even though he had publicly urged them to stay on, some might feel that this was only a kind of genial sham on the part of the new President. Thus, for one illustration, while his desk was piled with a hundred problems and visitors to his office were coming and going like men moving through a revolving door, he thought of Theodore Sorenson, the one who had been closest of all to the late President, and said to him: "Ted, I would like you to write the first draft of my first speech to Congress." It was an accolade to a suffering man, to whom Johnson, of course, gave the gist of what he intended to say.

3

THE NEW MAN

THAT SPEECH, DELIVERED ON WEDNES-day, November 27, was a most poignant one. For Johnson was returning to the forum in which he had served so long, first in the House of Representatives and then in the Senate; which he had, in his years there, embodied and mastered and "played upon like a violinist," as Senator Thomas Dodd of Connecticut once said. It was one of the most powerful men of Congress in its century and three-quarters of life who was now coming back to assert a new form of leadership over it. And assert leadership Johnson did, blandly, calmly, but determinedly, in what he called not a "State of the Union" message but only "remarks of the President."

Predictably, he promised to carry on the Kennedy program—notably in regard to civil rights, to which he gave a priority actually higher than the late President had been able to demand. But beyond this Johnson reassured the Congress, a large and often intractable public institution, just as he had reassured the private men, like Sorenson. He told Congress, in effect, that while he would demand and demand of it, he would always respect its constitutional independence and integrity. Kennedy had done no less, but justly or unjustly, although he was liked by Congress, he had never so deeply impressed the body in which he had sat in a junior place as had Johnson.

This was a most important speech, wholly apart from the sense of tragedy and timelessness—the timelessness of the institutions of this government, whatever loss and shock may come among the men who operate them. For Johnson was telling his old colleagues, as shortly he demonstrated to many of them in individual talks, that while he loved their institution and acknowledged all its proper perquisites, he was on to that institution, too. He knew when and over what matters it had a right to ponder long: but he also knew when and over what matters it could and should move fast. There would be more movement now; this was the burden of it all. And the message employed that method which is, at bottom, Johnson's fundamental political technique.

It is a technique which, despite his seemingly aggressive outer personality, depends more on understatement than overstatement. And it depends far more on head-to-head persuasion, with those who really matter in a given issue or problem, than on large, generalized appeal to the public. Thus, a Johnson talk with Senator Harry F. Byrd of Virginia, the powerful, honorable, and often quite immovable conservative leader on financial affairs, within an hour produced a much improved climate for the Kennedy tax reduction bill to which, just before his death, the late President had given highest place for the current session of Congress.

How are these things done? They are not done by large threats. A Byrd of Virginia could never, in ten or a hundred vis-à-vis meetings with a President, be frightened from any course on which he had set himself, and a Johnson would never suppose he could be. The President angrily and rightly rejects puerile interpretations of his capacity to negotiate as a capacity to rule through fear or bluster. Nor does his power lie in large promises. He did not pledge to Byrd all the federal "economy" that the Senator would really have liked as a precondition to a tax cut, but he showed to his old friend (and, on many issues, his friendly enemy) a determination to make *some* progress in budget-cutting. For Byrd, this was enough. It was not enough to alter a single one of his principles, but it showed that on the presidential side resolute and *effective* steps were being taken at least to approach that degree of governmental frugality which lies deep in the honest heart of that honest Senator.

One of these effective steps was Johnson's decision to cut his first federal budget below $100 billions, whereas it had been heading toward perhaps $104 billions. There was much understandably skeptical talk about new brooms and good intentions. But he did it. He did it by immersing himself for days and nights in that most dull and technical of all indispensable things, the budget estimates. He did it by calling in Cabinet officers, one at a time, and demanding that they justify in detail this or that item. If he became satisfied of its soundness the item would stay in, for Johnson is not a penny-pincher.

He has never been for economy simply for economy's sake. Nor does he really think that a balanced budget is the highest, or even the second highest, duty of a national leader. Thrift to him is a sound thing; but not a religion.

Still he has been around Washington a very long time; and like a veteran home office newspaper auditor, he knows all the dodges there are for padding accounts. Every Cabinet officer in the end not only cut his own budget but, upon reflection, agreed to the soundness of the cut toward which he had been pressed by the President's determination in which the less kind arts of persuasion were fully and frankly applied.

He was hardest of all with the military people, and with the very man in the Cabinet he most respects, Secretary of Defense Robert S. McNamara. For a lifelong career as a preparedness leader has taught Johnson that military strength is not automatically synonymous with spending. The factor of sheer waste is undeniably high. So he and McNamara, working in tandem as two hard realists, went after waste in ordering closed more than one hundred no longer indispensable American military bases and installations. It was the most pitilessly deep cut ever made by an American President in the most sensitive of all areas to members of Congress. For military installations bring not merely federal money but also a certain cachet to American communities, particularly to small ones. Traditionally they have been untouchable; for Congress defends its prerogatives in this matter with grim ferocity. For the President it was a most delicate operation. Not only was he offending congressional privilege and congressional codes of conduct and hitting at some of his oldest friends and former colleagues, he was also running a naked and undeniable political risk.

He was at this moment a very new President finishing out the term of another. Though he was to be a candidate for nomination in his own right only a few months hence, he had no personal Johnson organization within the national Democratic Party. Such party apparatus as existed was, inevitably, still a Kennedy apparatus. Though by no means in revolt against Johnson as Kennedy's heir, it was nevertheless a cadre which owed him no special allegiance and which he must win over in spirit as well as in form against the coming Democratic national convention of August, 1964.

All these factors were painfully relevant to the decision to close the redundant bases. McNamara, who rightly sees as his job to run the defense establishment and let others run the politics, had during Kennedy's time in office coldly and purposefully honed his axe against just these bases. The late President, however, had drawn back at the last moment and so suspended McNamara's cutting tool in mid-air. When Johnson allowed him to let it fall he took an action which according to any objective criterion was entirely sound, but on any political criterion was risky, indeed.

Many congressmen endlessly talk "economy," as many were doing at this precise moment. But, being human, they talk of economy for other people, other districts, other states. The outcry which greeted the new cuts both in Congress and in the communities and states affected was hard on the President's highly sensitive political eardrums. But, worse yet, five of the states hardest hit happened also to be five of the biggest and most critical states, in terms of electoral-vote strength. Three of them, New York, Illinois and Texas, had gone Democratic in the 1960 election, putting the Kennedy-Johnson administration under undeniable obligation. The other two, California and Ohio, had gone Republican in '60 and were high on President Johnson's private "must" list for carrying in '64.

In all these circumstances the President was, indeed, "putting in his stack" with McNamara. Still, he was far from terrified at the outcome, nor did he stand with his Secretary of Defense solely because he was convinced that the Secretary was right. He also took the line he did because, regarding McNamara as absolutely indispensable to his administration, and knowing quite well that the Secretary was not bound to him with those thongs of deep affection that had tied him to Kennedy, he wanted to give McNamara an early and unforgettable example of the Johnson capacity to give a valuable subordinate not only much chivvying but also much loyalty.

For one of the lessons Johnson had learned in the House was that unelected aides to politicians, of the kind he himself had once been to Congressman Kleberg, need not only the support of their bosses but their positive and unshakable protection in time of need. The political patron has to be a good and faithful patron.

To discuss President Johnson's unexampled skill in softening opposition to whatever he may wish to do is to consider a subtle, highly human thing, very difficult to describe in exact, measured and measurable terms. Many have pictured the President as simply a thrusting, all-demanding, political "operator" constantly twisting the arms, slapping the backs and befuddling the minds of his vis-à-vis. This interpretation substitutes hard-used stereotypes for competence to describe adequately a complex and subtle procedure. It is an interpretation about as silly as it would be to say that Heifetz is a great violinist because he has massive determination and very long hands with which to clutch his instrument and so beat grace and melody out of it.

Presidential negotiations with other powerful politicians—who are also invariably men with quite adequate respect for their own powers and positions—are not ever made on any such basis of footling, simplistic melodrama.

The bottom factor of Johnson's "operation" is a kind of specially informed power of persuasion, a persuasion which he will not attempt to use on small issues. The thing at issue must be national or international in scope, a major bill or a question of public policy.

Granted such a problem, the President first ponders all possible outcomes of it. There will be the best possible solution (rarely in fact attained in this imperfect world). There will be a desirable if less than perfect solution. There will be, perhaps, a less desirable but still better-than-nothing solution. Then, finally, there will be the quite intolerable possible solution—the total rejection of the bill or the policy in hand.

In his mind, the President begins at the bottom of this scale; at first his sole concern is to draw his consultants totally and irrevocably away from the worst possible solution; the quite intolerable one. This he will do by calmly and deliberately throwing them intellectually off-balance, a process of which he is master, combining both high audacity on his part and understanding of his consultant's view. For an illustration, say he is dealing with civil rights legislation and his audience is one or more powerful deep southern senators. He will say to them in substance: "Now, I understand your problems; I know that from where you sit you cannot vote for an all-out civil rights bill and remain alive politically. In me, you are not dealing with some fellow who is eagerly urging you to commit political suicide. But I know you to be reasonable men, and responsible men. I concede that you cannot go all the way with me here. Still, I know and you know that we must do something in this country about this problem; this is not because *I* am saying it; it is because history is saying it—and you know it is saying it. We are talking together as reasonable men, and all of us love and value our country. So I know you are not now going to say to me that you will accept nothing whatever in this field.

"A senator owes a duty to his state and to the opinions, and even prejudices of its people; and you know that I know this. But, after all, a senator is, in the end, a senator of the United States—*all* the United States."

All this will be said with gravity but also with the occasional interjection of Johnsonian humor which has thrown some of the most sophisticated men in this country off stride—and thus off the initiative. (A mutual friend once said smilingly to President Kennedy: "No man alive, in my judgment, ever entirely won any face-to-face argument with Lyndon Johnson; ever came out of one feeling as absolutely sure of his position as when he entered." Kennedy replied, with a grin: "How right! How right!")

President Johnson's humor, in these exchanges, and, indeed, generally, is principally a sense of the ridiculous, the grotesque.

Once, while he was pushing a bill as Senate minority

leader while the redoubtable Taft, as majority leader, was heading the opposition and also receiving the bulk of the current press coverage, Johnson personally telephoned a close friend who was then the Senate correspondent of a large metropolitan newspaper.

"Mr. So and So," his voice came blandly and very formally over the wire, "this is Lyndon Johnson; the minority leader of the Senate, you may remember. I would take it very kindly if I could have an appointment with the Senate correspondent of Such and Such. Now, of course, I don't want to put you out—I would be glad to meet you in Senator Taft's office."

This was his means of saying several things without quite saying any of them: That he had a sound reason to think that the favorable side of his bill was not being properly reported; that he thought undue attention was being paid to the opposing side, granting that a majority leader normally and properly is paid more press attention; that he was, however, not exactly complaining, just making a wistful little joke. There was no anger in his voice; only the smallest trace of sorrow and disappointment.

With just such quick thrusts of humor he has handled many a bill and many a problem; for to such there is, in the nature of things, no real rebuttal.

At all events, once he has isolated and destroyed, by the appeal of logic and reason and also by the swift, perhaps illogical but nevertheless efficacious use of unanswerable wit, the quite intolerable solution to his bill or program or plan, he moves against the half-loaf solution. For a very important distinction, however, he does not now bring into play his weapon of ridicule, or the deadpan kind of irony that often accompanies it. Here, now that he has very much softened up his audience of one or more (he is always most effective when his audience is five at most), he simply renews and extends the bargaining process by which he has won the first round.

Having brought about the destruction of the intolerable solution, he proceeds, now with much greater care, to show the manifest difficulties and shortcomings of the half-loaf solution. He stops just short of characterizing it as hopelessly foolish; for it may be that he will, after all, have to retreat in due course to this line as the only viable way left open. Given luck and circumstances he may at length dispose of half-loaf just as earlier he had disposed of quite-intolerable.

If so, at this point the drama of persuasion becomes more intense on the inside—inside Johnson—precisely as it seems to lessen in intensity on the outside. For here begins what is both the most critical and the most difficult to describe of all his techniques. As he called in his loans for Kennedy in the South in 1960, he begins now, in this hypothetical but essentially real example of how he works, to call in other loans, but less explictly than he called them in down South. As majority leader he did much for other senators; there was hardly a man on the Democratic side who did not owe him a debt of gratitude for a small kindness at the right time or a vital kindness at a desperately necessary time. As chairman of the Senate Democratic Steering Committee—one of the several hats he wore as majority leader—he had a large hand in the assignments of senators to legislative committees. He used this hand to place more new and promising senators in more truly important committee seats than had ever before been allowed the freshmen. The present Senate majority leader, Senator Mike Mansfield of Montana, went on the famous Foreign Relations Committee, one of the most sought-after in all the Senate, the very week he came up to that body from the House of Representatives. Senator Eugene McCarthy of Minnesota reached the puissant Finance Committee by similar Johnson interventions in his behalf. And so on, courtesy of LBJ.

Moreover, in 1954, when Vice-President Richard Nixon for the Republicans was leading a savage attack on the Democratic Party, it was Lyndon Johnson who bore a great share of the burden of a Democratic campaign which brought returned Democratic control of the Senate in the teeth of the then unexampled popularity of Dwight Eisenhower. Half a dozen Democratic senators, at least, owed him much when the smoke had cleared.

Liens of loyalty and affection and of respect—of such are made the irresistible ammunition in political wars. And Johnson has always known how to use them; but to use them decently and sensitively. He *demands* nothing of any man—certainly nothing in any way demeaning his self-respect. He does, sometimes, ask him for that extra effort, that extra personal risk possibly, when immense legislative battles are involved. He has done it since he has been in the White House, as so often he had done it before.

Moreover, his power of persuasion, though resting on many factors, rests most of all upon what is, to other politicians, the basic factor of all. He will never ask a political lieutenant to take a risk he will not take himself; he will never ask an exertion which he himself does not over-match. He is a combat political leader in the sense that some generals are combat generals. He is always up front, sometimes cussing and struggling, like Maurice Rose, who was always up front in hurling the Third Armored Division across France and Belgium and into Germany. His command post is invariably the farthest advanced in the forward line.

Political leadership is not in every way dissimilar to military leadership; for both depend in the end on the willing bodies and minds of men, and upon that infinitely subtle thing called morale, or *esprit de corps*. Johnson, in this analogy, is a Jeb Stuart with a plume in his hat. But he is, also and at the same time, something else altogether. He is, in one part of his personality as a leader, a Bernard Montgomery. The old Field Marshal, one of the great British soldiers of this century, was unutterably demanding of those about him, and full of the will to fight. But he never confused the will to fight with a willingness to make himself a personal hero by vain and bloody charges against impossible obstacles, simply so that later men could say "Monty never retreated."

Thus with Johnson. He is not interested and never has been interested in losing battles. For him there is only an embarrassingly sentimental, stickily precious, absurdity in some hopeless charge which only courts certain doom for his troops and his cause. In 1952 when the late Senator Joseph McCarthy was making a shambles of orderly process, and a shambles of the lives of some of his victims, Johnson burned in cold inner anger. He knew what McCarthy was doing to this country, and frantically sought

a means to halt it. But he knew also that he had not at
hand the troops to counterattack and would not have
them until McCarthy had at least overreached himself.

Liberal senators, whose indignation did them credit
but whose lack of realism could have brought a disaster,
merely entrenching and increasing McCarthy's virulent
influence, pressed for an immediate showdown. Stolidly,
Johnson restrained them, as Montgomery restrained eager
staff officers from premature action in the north of Nor-
mandy. "Wait," he said, "Wait."

At this point one of his journalistic friends went to
him and said: "Something, somebody, has got to stop this
man McCarthy. You simply must now put the Democratic party on the attack against him." He smiled sadly,
and replied: "You want McCarthyism brought down; I
want McCarthyism brought down. But to go after him
now will end in certain disaster; we have not now got the
votes to condemn him. If we try now, it will be blazoned
to all the world that the Senate of the United States is
helpless before him. And so, at this moment, we are.
For now, he will win. We will not attack him until *we*
can win; to do anything else would play into his hands
as nothing has ever done. I will not destroy the Democratic Party and the United States Senate by letting the
world see both at McCarthy's knees.

"We will beat him, all right; but it will take time. Some
of the storm in the public mind must pass first. He has so
oversimplified things, his followers have so oversimplified
things, that if we attack him now it will be thought that
the Senate is afraid of his disclosures; that we are silenc-
ing a man warning the people against Communism. I will

not commit my party to some high school debate on the subject 'Resolved that Communism is good for the United States,' with my party taking the affirmative."

In due time, Johnson engaged McCarthy and defeated him. It was Johnson's achievement, personally, to an almost incredible degree. The operative phrase to him, however, was "in due time," meaning at the effective time.

Some years later, the writer told this story to the late Hugh Gaitskell, leader of the Labor Party in England. Gaitskell smiled and said: "I have got here a thing that tells you how right I think Johnson was. On my desk is a report from a Royal Commission proposing some easing of our very cruel laws dealing with homosexuality. I *know* these laws are too harsh; I *know* they ought to be altered. But I couldn't win, my party couldn't win, that fight just now. And I am not going to commit my party to the proposition that homosexuality is good for the British Isles— and the Labor Party. Politics, old man, and indeed all public affairs, must rest on timing. Sometimes the seemingly 'good' thing to do is the very worst thing you could try; because, in a free society, you must sometimes first have public consent to do even the most manifestly good thing. And, sometimes, you must not, you dare not, fail to obtain that consent. For, at these times, failing to obtain it is even worse—far worse—than the manifest ill you would like to cure. For then you see your party and country committed, right out in public, in a free choice, to what you know to be a monstrous evil."

Thus, in Johnson's method of operation, and in his own personality, there is a constant tug of war between restraint and go-get-'em; between the cool approach of plan-

ning and reason and the hot approach of damn the tor-
pedoes and all that. The cool approach invariably wins
in the end because he knows, as all really good English
and American politicians know, that the great, real drama
of government is never a confrontation between the ab-
solutes of good and bad, sound and unsound, wise and unwise. Instead, it is a far less tidy drama destined to end,
cliché though this is, in the greatest *possible* good for the
greatest possible number—*not* in the perfect good which
is unattainable in a highly imperfect world.

4

WHAT MANNER OF MAN?

PRESIDENT JOHNSON'S DISTRUST OF doctrinaire solutions to political problems, and of absolute, all-or-nothing stands which are good theater but bad politics, is not merely a matter of taste. It is also the fruit of hard experience in a hard trade constantly bedeviled, in every free society, by the certainty and sense of personal rightness and self-righteousness which are the hallmarks of political extremism. In a word, his politics makes performance, and not assertion, its ultimate goal.

This being the fact, he is often put down as the Great Compromiser by some who honestly believe in a politics of the absolute and regard any departure from this concept as "maneuvering" and abandonment of principle.

For years, the far-liberal wing of the Democratic Party felt this way. And when Kennedy took the decision at the 1960 Democratic national convention to make Johnson his running mate there were cries of bitterness and hostility from ultra-liberal delegates whose emotions were not soon soothed even by Kennedy, who had insisted upon this arrangement.

It was an old story to Johnson. The right had habitually fought him, at home in Texas and in the Senate; the left had habitually fought him, at home in Texas and in the Senate. Their blows hurt him always; but notably those from the left, for he knew that the animosity of the right was often at least logical. He has always had an intellectual kinship with liberalism along with a special, personal fondness for many of the representatives in public affairs of American conservatism, such as the southerners in the Senate and House.

Johnson's association with them all through his public years has been one of the strangest stories in recent American politics. Physically and geographically, he is a southerner. In emotion, in basic point of view, in personal background he is the westerner he said he was in 1960, to a good deal of jeering from cynics who thought he was only avoiding a politically dangerous label. Still, in the literal sense he was a southerner, and from the start of his career in Congress, a member of that powerful, clannish lodge which is the South-in-Congress. One is born to that state, much as one is born, say, an Episcopalian, and this is a lodge from which, once in, it is almost impossible to be expelled.

He never at any time made any bones to his southern Congressional friends of the fact that he was not really a southerner in their definition, which includes qualities and attitudes far more subtle than the factor of geography. This was not truly the way he was, or the way he had been brought up. But the old southern fellows, such as the late Senator Walter George of Georgia, only smiled among themselves and said, "Well, yes, of course Lyndon *is* different; but anyhow he is—well he is just Lyndon." It was said of the late Senator Alben Barkley of Kentucky that while he consistently violated most of Kentucky's ideas about politics, Kentucky with equal consistency kept quite inconsistently returning him to office. Why? Well, "Kentucky just *understood* old Alben."

It has always been much the same with Johnson and the southerners in Congress; they "just *understood* ol' Lyndon." They have always "understood" him—which is to say easily tolerated and generally supported him—in spite of the fact that his voting record, taking it all in all, is profoundly at variance with the common southern voting record, and not merely on matters like civil rights. As a performing politician, indeed, and putting aside the almost glandular objection to him of ultra-liberals for not *talking* a better game, the Johnson liberal index is high. Taking it all in all, and making allowance for the fact that the late President's was not so long, Johnson's liberal voting record is at least as high as that of John F. Kennedy, and covers all that complex of issues ordinarily used to measure who is politically liberal and who conservative: public power, public housing, aid to education, minimum wage, medical aid, pensions and so on.

In politics, however, manner is nearly as important as matter, and what are called "public images" can become as important as either or both. By 1960, Johnson wanted to seek the presidential nomination but was so long restrained from openly jousting for it by the necessities of his post as Senate majority leader that the belated campaign was an impossibly uphill fight. At this time ultra-liberals threw about him a totally false "public image."

He had, in 1957, caused the United States Senate to adopt the first substantial civil rights bill in the eight decades since Reconstruction, and first step, half-loaf bill though it was, it required the most exquisitely skilled leadership to get it passed. Yet in 1960, he was presented in the liberal image as a "mere operator" in legislation.

The fact that John Kennedy had voted just as Johnson had voted in all the critical phases of this long Senate struggle did not prevent Kennedy's being credited, again by the ultra-liberals, with a sincerity of purpose. The fact was that Johnson, a Texan, had become the first and only Senate leader since the Civil War to challenge and to defeat, on this harsh and bitter issue, the massed southern forces to whom his heart was alleged, against all demonstrable proof, somehow to belong. Against the open record of the Senate's action, the man who at great risk to himself had forced upon his own section of the country this historic legislation for human equality was dismissed by his ultra-liberal critics as a maneuverer.

On and on went this disregard of the facts. The man who in Texas had been invariably and bitterly opposed by the most powerful and richest of the conservative forces of the state—including the oil interests until he became so influential and entrenched in Congress that they perforce made their peace with him—was presented in the North and East as a cartoonist's figure of the southern Bourbon.

His brilliance as Senate leader had to be accepted, since it was undeniable even within the context of unthink. But it was waved aside with the observation that while Johnson was, perhaps, "an activist," he was not, poor fellow, a "thinker" or an "innovator." This reflected two things: first, an incredible belief that political "action" is not what of course it is, an extension of political thought, philosophy and planning, and second, a technique by which Johnson's detractors could catch him either way. Whenever he did not perform as Senate leader as rapidly as they wished or in the way they wished, they accused him of complicity with the conservative coalition of Republicans and southern Democrats—as quite inadequate as an activist. When he performed too rapidly, too effectively, they sighed that here was a man who only moved and never reflected; he was a kind of wild Texas steer loose in the fine, precious galleries of intellectualism.

This amazing nonsense long occupied the minds of some otherwise perfectly sensible people. It was primarily a syndrome of the ultra-liberals, who reacted emotionally and irrationally against Johnson and Johnson's personality in almost exact proportion to the depth of their debt to him as a Senate leader who habitually saved them and their designs from the most humiliating and jejune of follies and ineffectualness. The more he did for them and for liberalism, the more they disliked him. The more he carried forward their own programs, after altering them to make them tolerable to the concurrently effective majority of the Senate, the more they accepted the political benefit to themselves while sneering at the man who had brought those benefits about.

To add to the irony of all this, the *effective* and rational liberals, such men as Senators Hubert Humphrey and Eugene McCarthy and Ernest Gruening and Henry Jackson and Warren Magnuson, came to understand, support and value Johnson as their friend and ultimate protector. Just so, the *effective* right wingers, from Robert Taft's time and beyond, always knew him for what he was: the strongest antagonist they had, precisely *because he knew how to make rational liberalism work* and they knew he did. These right-wingers never feared the shouting, talking liberals who lacked the capacity to turn a set of slogans into a bill, a program, or a policy.

Johnson's position with the ultra-liberals was not unlike that of the apocryphal American lend-lease inspector in Russia during the war. Lend-lease had provided an enormous plant, plus all the materials, plans and other necessary aids, for the construction of fighter bombers. The visiting inspector found these turned out by the hundreds, glistening in their new paint and ready to go, but for one small omission. "But Commissar," he said in pained perplexity after looking into a dozen of the aircraft, "where are the engines?"

"Ah," said the Commissar to the American. "I thought you'd ask that. Well, what about those lynchings in the South?"

It was in these circumstances that Johnson for years worked in such patient fortitude as he could muster. Not unnaturally, it was a deeply pained fortitude. For, like all men, he does not relish being misunderstood and misrepresented, and certainly not with that dogged persistence that was so long his lot. Even more than the hostility of his critics, he resented what to him is one of life's most intolerable things—irrationality in anything, of any nature, that may confront him. All that saved him, perhaps, from a final conviction that the world had gone mad was his somewhat mordant sense of humor.

One evening at a small dinner party, where he was an exhausted guest after a sixteen-hour working day driving through the Senate a small bill dearly beloved by the more theatrical liberals, he sat silent for a long time while some of his fellow guests offered him no thanks but only a brisk critique pointing out how much better he might have done the job. To their words of advice, not un-mixed with a spirit of brittle condemnation, he made no reply. At length, perhaps remembering that after all he *had* brought their bill through an essentially hostile chamber, one of them asked him, in order to turn the subject: "Senator, by the way, whom do you regard as the best single associate in the Senate for your leadership?"

Johnson examined the question with great gravity, pulling at his chin thoughtfully and seemingly going over in his mind the whole long list of his senatorial colleagues. "Why," he said at last, "as you would suppose, I have given that question a great deal of thought over the years. And I have come to the conclusion that the one man who is most helpful of all to me is Senator Malone." George Malone of Nevada, a right-wing Republican, had for years been the most devoted, most single-minded, antagonist the Democratic Party had to meet daily in the Senate.

It was his awareness of the capacity for mischief to-ward the Democratic legislative program of the Malones of the Senate—and also of the Democratic ultra-liberals —which at this precise moment was preventing Johnson from undertaking the only pre-convention campaign for the 1960 presidential nomination that could conceivably have won for him—an open, candid, all-out run for it, early on. Instead, he had to move only obliquely, feeling that he owed it to his party, to its program and to the Senate itself not to become a positive opponent to Senator Kennedy or to Senator Stuart Symington of Missouri, who then was also actively in the running. "The country can't stand, the party can't stand, the Senate can't stand having three active presidential candidates in the Senate—of whom one is the majority leader," he told a friend. "I simply cannot be a real candidate; I can't get away from here to do all the speech-making and delegate-hunting that would be necessary. I have simply got to stay here and mind the store."

To associates who persistently urged him to go all-out he at first turned a sympathetic if still rejecting ear; he appreciated the compliment, and he knew they wished him well. But as this sort of pressure went on and on he became deeply annoyed. And with Johnson, as always, that also meant openly annoyed. He had a very low point of tolerance for this pressure, even when it was most genial and kindly intentioned. To him it was quite obvious why the majority leader should not be in a personally demanding role before the convention met. He assumed it was obvious to others. At any rate, he typically would not make a long, patient explanation of his conduct.

"I don't push worth a damn," he once said, meaning that when anyone begins to shove at him, whether from the best or the worst of motives, he angrily digs in and will not move. But, apart from all this, though he seems extroverted and outgoing, he has a powerful sense of personal reticence and privacy and an active notion of decorum in public affairs.

Openly and unashamedly he values, respects and enjoys high public office, and openly and unashamedly he enjoys its perquisites while bearing its burdens. He has never in his life made a poor-mouth, poor-me, little-old-log-cabin-fellow, campaign for what is called by some politicians "the sympathy vote." Habitually, whatever the office he has sought, he has gone among his constituents in deliberate grandeur, in the biggest car he may have and in the finest clothes. He does not want people to weep for him or to hold him in fond pity; he wants them to respect him, his strength and his position, and to vote for him out of belief that he is not a "common man," as, indeed, most definitely he is not. Though he is one of the most urgent vote-gatherers of his time, there is not an ounce of demagogy in him.

His personal reticence makes him detest explaining himself or his motives. And he has a profound unwillingness to discuss anything that he considers to be his private affair. He never accuses any other public man of evil motives, though he will bridle angrily and unhesitatingly denounce what he may feel to be a *petty* motive. He expects, in his turn, not to be accused of evil motives, though in fact, of course, he has many times as a professional politician been so accused. But no one ever indicted him for littleness.

It was most of all Johnson's personal reticence—not so unusual a quality in a politician as many people suppose —that caused much confusion about his purposes in 1960.

Not until the very end, not until Congress had adjourned and he could leave the Senate in a state of shuttered quiet and the legislative program finished, did he start the usual actions of a presidential candidate. By then it was far too late, as in his heart he himself had known it would be. And sometimes—indeed, a good part of the time—he really did not want to make the effort at all.

In the meantime his sense of irony served to give him a certain philosophic resignation and, occasionally, even a certain sardonic private amusement. During this pre-convention period, when those who knew Johnson well knew he did not want to hash over the situation, a very young foreign diplomat, a guest at a party in the home of one of Johnson's friends, rushed in and demanded of the then Senate majority leader:

"Sir, what are your *real* presidential ambitions?" Johnson looked at him with a glint in the eye, but with impassive face and manner, and replied: "My highest ambition of all is to help elect *some other man President,* in the hope that maybe he would make me his appointments secretary."

This was a not uncommon instance of the dry humor with which often he meets questions he regards as uninformed or childish, the only kinds of questions that truly annoy him. It was the same, incidentally, with his old friend and frequent antagonist, the late Senator Robert A. Taft. Taft could tolerate any number of hard and even harsh questions, in press conferences or from hecklers in political meetings, but not the kind of question that struck him as puerile. To this sort of thing, he returned a freezing, open contempt, and like as not he would not reply at all.

Johnson, on the contrary, will always reply. But he cannot readily master his sense of the absurd, and this gets him, sometimes, into difficulties and has led on occasion to the charge that he is both impatient and arrogant. He is undeniably impatient but only arrogant in not relishing the company or conversation of foolish people, or the burden of repetitive nonsense. Quickly intuitive and perceptive, he has both the strength and the weakness of most artists, his art being that of politics. He is weak in understanding that many others are not as perceptive as he is. Being quick to pity, he is equally quick to scorn. He dislikes "drawing pictures and diagrams," persisting in the assumption, often quite unfounded, that sensible men will understand his purposes without being told, just as he would, in fact, understand theirs.

Being an artist, he is temperamental, both inside and outside his craft. Highly professional, he is not charitable toward amateurs wherever they do not frankly concede that status, though he can be infinitely patient with those who make no pretense of expertise. If a man claims to be a pro, whether a politician, a political writer, a government or congressional employee, Johnson assumes that he will act as one and is most displeased if he does not.

All through the years, therefore, while he was in Congress, in the Vice-Presidency, and, now, in the Presidency, his staff has been kept incessantly at that fever pitch at which he himself habitually operates. He tolerates nothing slipshod; he bellows for results, he drives the staff hard, but to all of them he is sensitively kind. When a staff man is ill and Johnson learns of it he personally calls the best physician and arranges for the best hospitalization to be had. Over the years he has helped dozens of his people to buy their own homes; he frets endlessly about their well-being and the well-being of their children. He will turn from the gravest of state issues to say to a stenographer, "You are not looking well; I am worried about your weight. Now, you must do thus and so."

His people, although the hardest working staff in Washington, are loyal to the boss. The President has, for all who are in any way close to him, a strong paternalistic feeling. No matter what his own position has been, his staff members have always been almost literally within the family. They could be found at the most opulent of Johnson dinner parties and also at the most intimate of suppers, at Christmastime, Thanksgiving, or whatever. When Mrs. Johnson took the family cook with her to hear the new President's first address to Congress, she was simply doing what came naturally.

At any given occasion before he was President—though this cannot all be true now that he is in the White House—one could expect to see staff people of any rank in one of his offices. On their side, the staff have always been relaxed socially with the President. Johnson's principal assistant is Walter Jenkins. On the day the Johnsons moved into the White House, Mrs. Marjorie Jenkins said to Walter-Jenkins (the President, who is always in a hurry, often calls him thus, as though his Christian name and surname were joined into a single name) that she thought it would be difficult for Mrs. Johnson, going into a new house and having to bother about dinner.

The Walter-Jenkinses therefore invited the Lyndon Johnsons to supper at the Jenkins home in Northwest Washington and the Johnsons came along without giving the matter a thought. Mrs. Jenkins, of course, knew that there were cooks in the White House and that the Johnsons no doubt could have scared up a small meal on their own. Still, she did what seemed natural to her, and the Johnsons did what seemed natural to them.

Johnson's personal success with his staff, to whom he needs to make no explanations, has not always been paralleled by success in his dealings with a part of the national press. Here, too, men of ultra-liberal and ultra-rightest viewpoint have often joined in hostility toward him. Some of the press has never forgiven him for being from Texas, which to them is positively redolent of an evil thing called "oil." Some of the press has never forgiven him for having gone to a little freshwater teachers' college in Texas instead of to an Ivy League university. One critic, indeed, has observed that because of this, Johnson could not be a profound thinker. The difference in intellectual content between the Kennedy administration and the Johnson administration, he said, could readily be measured: John Kennedy had gone to Harvard—and look, pray, where Lyndon Johnson had gone.

Some of the press, quite simply, has never forgiven him —though this sounds extreme—for another reason for which some of the ultra-liberals in the Senate have never forgiven him. This is the circumstance that, over so many years and against every article of their still somewhat collegiate old grad faith, he has so demonstrably, so repeatedly and so infuriatingly casually, out-thought and out-acted their own heroes from "backgrounds" so eminently more suitable in their eyes. So they have presented him, alternately, as a dark and brooding figure of "manipulation," up to God knows what tricky maneuvers, and as a large, awkward, simple rustic from Texas, from some dreadful little cow college, with manure on his boots and a ten-gallon hat perpetually cocked on a most cocky head.

Because all this was so callow, so *silly*, Johnson finds it difficult to credit that any political journalism could be based on criteria which he would regard as for "little boys." The phrase "little boys," means to him arrested development. It is one of the most cutting in his lexicon, applicable only to a special kind of folly—not plain folly but folly proceeding from a juvenile snobbery of which he is only vaguely, and with enormous scorn, aware.

"One of the strangest things I have ever observed about Lyndon," an old Senate colleague once said, "is the fact that he never thinks about 'protecting' himself." By this he meant that it has never yet entered Johnson's head that he needs, in any circumstances, to be anything but himself. When he is bored, he shows it, anywhere, anytime. When he is hungry he eats, though Mrs. Johnson keeps after him pretty well in this regard, since he tends to overweight, especially about the middle. He is not and never could be a buttoned-up kind of man and he has never been careful about his personal "image." He cannot bear excessive concern for his physical safety; similarly, he is at times too unconcerned for his political safety. When he does a "good" thing politically he does not take pains to see that all will quickly learn of it; he is vain enough but his vanity does not run in this direction.

In 1952 he was the first elected politician in Texas to come out openly for the Democratic presidential nominee of that year, Adlai E. Stevenson, who was unpopular in the state and was quite plainly on the road to defeat there. He met Stevenson at the state line and campaigned all across Texas with him. His reward, in some of the ultra-liberal press, was the persistently circulated rumor that "Lyndon didn't go for Stevenson." His mistake had been that he did not seek out the right people at the right time to tell them what he thought was obvious: that he *had*, quite demonstrably and beyond any possibility of doubt, gone all the way for Stevenson.

"When I do something," he said later of this episode, "I figure I am dealing with grown-up people. I'll be damned if I am ever going around with a sandwich board on my back reading: 'Look what I, Lyndon Johnson, have done for Stevenson.'"

To some extent, indeed, his persistent failure to protect himself from the oversimplifications of others is his own fault. A man of ready sentiment, he at the same time flinches from any parade of emotions and, peculiarly, from any parade of noble intentions. Some of the most compassionate things he has done for people in his public life, notably by way of legislation he has steered through Congress, he has accomplished with a surface air of skepticism and even cynicism. Rather than being thought soft he prefers to be thought unduly hard.

When he has brought off, say, a bill to increase the minimum wage among the lowest-paid in the American economic structure he will speak of it as though it were primarily only a *tour de force* in political management. He does not say that his motivation was not really the desire to be a political "operator" but to make life a little better for many people. The impression is thus left among those who think in stereotypes that Johnson is concerned only with power and not very much with who will benefit from that power.

Over and over when he was leader of the Senate he would describe some legislative coup to correspondents with what can rightly be called a candor so excessive as to be wholly misleading, and wholly unfair to himself. Because he dislikes attitudinizing, particularly attitudinizing in behalf of "good" projects, he will describe even beyond the actual fact the urgently persuasive steps he has taken in behalf of such a project while totally neglecting even to intimate that his heart was in the job simply because in justice it was a job that must be done.

For years he has been deeply sensitive to the press generally, and sometimes, through circumstances, hypersensitive. Because he has been so often misunderstood and misrepresented by some reporters, he works too hard at gaining their total approval, or at least their total understanding. This attitude, based on a vexed private determination to "*make* those fellows get the point," led some reporters before he had been four months in the Presidency to declare that he was "courting the press." This was based on the fact that Johnson had made himself more accessible to individual correspondents than any President in history, not excepting Kennedy, who was also highly sensitive to press criticism but was nevertheless never much attacked for it by the ultra-liberal press, which automatically liked Kennedy much as it automatically disliked Johnson.

To be accused of "courting the press," sometimes for granting audiences to the very members of it who had asked for audiences, only heightened the "undue sensitivity" with which he was charged. So on his side Johnson would grip his brow at times in exasperation, and sometimes this exasperation would clearly show in his conferences with the press generally. It is a kind of small, not too important, vicious circle: Johnson at bottom does not well or willingly explain himself as a *person* but goes to vast lengths to explain his acts as *President*. The distinction, though not hopelessly subtle, is lost on some. And so the more he tries to operate in what is to him not a dichotomy but only a sensible distinction, the more it appears to some others to *be* a dichotomy.

This curious situation once led the highly competent and independent-minded columnist Betty Beale of the *Washington Star*—a lady who wears no man's collar and is terrified by no party or partisan interest—to make these observations in her paper:

It's a well-known Washington adage that no matter who occupies the White House they are damned if they do and damned if they don't.

But this columnist never thought she would live to see the day when the press criticized the President for being nice to the press! The press corps as a group has never before had it so good under any previous President. Perhaps there lies the rub.

The Lyndon Johnsons have not changed one iota since

entering the White House. They have always regarded reporters as people and they like and are kind to people they come in contact with—whether it's a camel driver on a dusty street in Karachi, a weary reporter in a cubby hole in the National Press Building, or a chancellor of a European state.

To reporters who were regarded with interest because of preferential treatment received from past Presidents, such an expansive warmth to all people—especially all reporters—is apparently so disenchanting as to be incomprehensible.

A welcome-to-all attitude only arouses their suspicions, if not contempt. The theory seems to be that nobody can be that nice, so it has to be basically wrong.

The fact that the President believes in talking to all the press, instead of a few; the fact that this President is the first to share his information and problems with all the Senate and the House, should arouse admiration for his efforts toward an informed electorate and unified government. All the Senators and Representatives seem to appreciate it; but not all the press. When only a few have the inside track, criticism is understandable. When everyone gets an even break, it is hard to see how anyone can find fault, but leave it to the press to find fault even with the generous attitude toward them.

Mrs. Johnson once called him "a practical idealist"; it is not an inexact description. Still, though he likes to be praised as much, perhaps, as any man, he is skittish about such terms as "idealist" in relation to himself.

Though he has done a great deal for "the little man"— in minimum wage, in rural electrification, in slum clearance, in public housing, in anti-discrimination in hiring —Johnson for years was generally seen as only the odd legislative force which brought to completion the designs of other men in these fields. This, again, is because he plays an infinitely better game than he talks. He is not eloquent, though on rare occasions he can speak the true idiom of America with poignant perception and skill, and, for a politician, he does not talk much at all.

In the Senate, his speeches were low-keyed, both in content and delivery, and sometimes he spoke in such soft tones that the official stenographers and the press gallery had difficulty in following him. Always his goal was action, achievement; and for this, too, he got into trouble with some of his critics, who saw him as too masterful altogether. Deeply fond of the Senate's traditions of leisurely debate, he is also aware, and always has been, that there can be quite too much of a good thing. Thus, as Senate leader he was at times brusque to the point of rudeness to colleagues who talked interminably; many a time he all but pulled down some famously verbose senator by his coattails.

Again, when he had spent days and sometimes weeks in bringing a great matter to the point of the decisive roll call, his thirst to see the job done would find him leaning forward in his seat like a leashed bird-dog, his eyes fixed urgently on the reading clerk. And as that official began the slow, stately call of the roll Johnson would half rise from his chair and violently sweep his hand in a circular motion, meaning "Get on with it! Get on with it!"

He did at times do things and say things, in his total determination to keep the Senate moving in coherent order, that bruised feelings in perhaps the most temperamental, most proud forum in the world. Many a dusty cobweb of custom and tradition there he blew away forever; and many a laggard or intellectually flatulent colleague suffered from his ridicule. Still, what he did *for* the Senate was immeasurably greater than what he did to it, and even those who had found him a bit too urgent had cause to miss him after he became Vice-President.

Quite undeniably, something went out of the United States Senate when Johnson had gone. Gone was that sense of action and achievement, sometimes glorious, always onward-looking, which "ole Lyndon" had invariably embodied. The clerks worked less; but unaccountably enjoyed it less too. The pages had more time to stand about; but were not made overly happy thereby. August senators themselves had more time for reflection; but less justification for pointing with pride at the end of any Senate session to what had been done. The scene was rather like one in which a gale had recently passed; the air was calmer, to be sure, but, by God, it was a lot duller, too.

It was, to use a military analogy, as though a famous division had suddenly lost its even more famous commander. Now, it was not chivvied and harried about. Now the old man was no longer pushing and pulling and darting about to every command post shouting orders— and sometimes curses—and thrusting the whole great company forward, accepting no excuses, allowing no gold-bricking and continually crying for attack and yet more attack by troops who thought that they were already exhausted. Those troops found, in the long lull that followed Johnson's elevation, that they had not really been quite so exhausted as they had thought. And they also found that the old man had been good for something more than driving them on; he had also been useful in fighting off the common enemies of them all. They found that there is no substitute for the power of command.

But Johnson, himself, as he kicked himself up those gilded stairs to the Vice-President's office, had a far more difficult adjustment to make than had his old comrades of the Senate. They missed his leadership, but he missed what had been until then his very life. His assigned constitutional functions were only two: to preside over the Senate, his voice now stilled in all of its debates, and to act for President Kennedy in such ways and at such times as the President might direct.

Many supposed that Johnson, given his personality, would simply continue to direct the Senate from upstairs. But they misjudged their man. He knew that the power he had formerly exercised was his no longer; he knew, too, that intrusion upon the new leadership headed by Mike Mansfield would be both graceless and disruptive of constitutional procedure. So he remained aloof. He was always available to the Mansfield leadership to assist— when asked, but at no other time. He was now a member not of the legislative but of the executive branch of the government; he well knew the distinction between the two and he had no intention of stepping over the boundary line.

On a few occasions—notably on foreign policy issues —Johnson moved into the fray, on invitation, and with great caution so as not to upset precedent and protocol. And on these occasions he was most useful. But he had entered upon the Vice-Presidency in full awareness that he could not be his own man anymore. So, for the most part, he simply presided over the Senate, giving no unsought advice even if sometimes he had to hold himself in as he saw an overlooked opening here for the Democrats, an unguarded sally port there for the counterattacking Republicans, which his instinct told him should be attended to without delay but about which his new position required him to keep silent.

5

JOHNSON AND
THE "KENNEDY MEN"

ALMOST, ONE THOUGHT, HE WAS overscrupulous; but he had determined, as he once put it, to be the best Vice-President who had ever served. It was an extraordinarily difficult thing; for he had been a superb first man and good first men rarely make good second men. Still, this was the road he had taken, and he meant to follow it, in conscience and in good heart, to the end. He was deeply sensitive to the fact that he *was* now a second man. And he was deeply concerned to make no statement, take no step, which could possibly be interpreted, in the profoundly, invariably and institutionally suspicious political community of Washington, as an effort to move in either on the prerogatives of his President, or of his old home, the Senate. He was truly grateful for the magnanimity habitually shown him by Kennedy, and absolutely determined to return, in full measure, his own generosity, trust and confidence.

Kennedy fully appreciated the delicacy and difficulty of Johnson's role; he once told me: "Lyndon's job is the hardest one he could ever have—and he is performing it like a man, M-A-N." Those who had predicted that a relationship putting the erstwhile junior ahead of the erstwhile senior would "never work" had misread both men. For one of the things that makes a man powerful in the first place is a sense of proportion, of reality and of history. Johnson knew when he said "yes" to Kennedy at the Los Angeles convention that he was saying goodbye, for a term of years at least, to the power and the glory of the past. He also knew, of course, that, given Kennedy's generally expected run of eight years in the White House, Lyndon Johnson's turn might then come—as also it might not.

When the cards turn against him, as they did at Los Angeles, and when his stack of chips has run out, he can never resent the *player* who held the winning hand. He does not tear up his IOUs. Without the slightest hesitation, he collected on behalf of Kennedy the IOUs of others who owed him much and Kennedy little. In his time as Vice-President he never uttered or permitted criticism of his chief, although he did not in heart approve of everything that Kennedy did, notably in the field of foreign policy. He showed this quickly when he himself became President.

There was, for illustration, the curt Johnson order, the moment he entered the White House, for an end of backbiting and cross-purposes in our diplomatic-military-intelligence mission in South Viet Nam, which had been sent to help the South Vietnamese fight invading Communists, but which sometimes seemed to be fighting instead within itself. There was, for another illustration, the fundamental overhaul under Thomas C. Mann of our policies toward Latin America, which had become bogged down by men who had a too doctrinaire approach to the Latins without understanding that their respect for this country must precede their affection for it. And there were other changes.

But none of Johnson's reservations implied in these changes of policy was ever mentioned by him, directly or indirectly, even to his closest friends, while he remained Vice-President. Another Texan, John N. Garner, had once said of his own President, Franklin D. Roosevelt: "He is my chief and I will follow his course. If it shall take him to political hell, I will be there at his elbow, sniffing the sulphurous fumes." Old Cactus Jack meant it; but as time went by he found it impossible to keep the pledge. Johnson never said it at all; for such a declaration would have been too orotund for his taste and too intrusive upon his private reserve. But he meant such a pledge, and he kept it.

As he gave repeated proof that he would keep it, Kennedy's confidence in his loyalty began to influence the lesser figures within the administration—notably in the White House Palace Guard—which had looked upon Johnson at the beginning with both suspicion and resentment.

The "intellectuals" within the old Administration began to see that the man from Texas was not without a profound political sophistication, though he would never suggest this himself. He would in fact often go out of his way to present himself as a sort of naively cheerful rural extrovert. And they began to see that the Vice-President was also truly "committed"—one of their favorite terms which he himself never used and from which he would sometimes flinch with a wry smile—to those programs, notably civil rights and public welfare, which before entering the government they had supposed to be quite outside the vision of so practical an operator.

They began to see that Johnson was to Kennedy about what a tough and able regular Army top sergeant may be to a younger lieutenant not too long out of West Point. They began to see him as an indispensable man who would never thrust his way into any Cabinet discussions but, who, once invited into it by the President, would put his points with a powerful, scarifying bluntness which at first slightly repelled and ultimately fascinated them.

It was a period—this tragically short three years of the Kennedy administration—of youth-worship in American politics. This was not because Kennedy had wanted it so but because those around him had become much more enchanted than he ever was with the notion that fate had ordained that the country could be got "moving again" by their generation alone.

Johnson was, in this sense, the odd man out. Though by no means leaning on a stick and holding an ear trumpet, he was in his fifties while Kennedy and most of the others were in their forties. It was the great time of the forty-year-olds; and they meant to make the most of it. One of them once told me, with a good deal of accuracy, that the men in their fifties were "the skipped generation." Those in their sixties who served the Kennedy administration were acceptable, he indicated, if only because everyone knew they had not much farther to go. But those in their fifties, so he suggested, were, by and large, "out" and not "in."

All this meant that while Johnson was in intimate association with his chief, and at length warily respected by his chief's White House assistants, there was not the relaxed, very human association between them and the Vice-

President that there was between him and Kennedy himself. There was very little of a Texan, or southwestern, or southern, atmosphere in the Kennedy administration; in this regard Johnson was an island alone amongst the President's entourage. To Johnson and Kennedy themselves, both being political pros, such fanciful conceits as skipped generations and human islands would never have occurred; such concepts lack substance and these two were both, pre-eminently and always, engaged with substance and not shadow. Kennedy no more cared about a man's age than about the color of his tie; seventy or thirty, it was all one to him if the man could do the job that needed to be done. Johnson no more cared about being a supposed western island in a hypothetical eastern sea than he did that some administration figures might suspect he was weak in his appreciation of the more subtle forms of Russian ballet.

Thus, when he himself came suddenly to power and many wondered aloud how long "the old White House crew" would stay on, Johnson was impatiently non-attentive. Some urged him to "make a clean sweep," suggesting that the old people could hardly serve him well, and that, anyhow, some of them had uttered slights about him in the past. In this, they were pushing at a twice-closed door with the new President. In the first place, he is a very difficult man to slight, and his self-confidence does not suggest to him that anyone would try it. The point was well illustrated, shortly after his accession to office, in his handling of the prickly President Charles de Gaulle of France. De Gaulle, who has made a curiously rewarding international political career out of a towering, somewhat irrational haughtiness, seemed to some to have snubbed Johnson as to when and where and in what circumstances the two presidents should meet. There was speculation in Washington, some of it audible, as to how Johnson would handle this supposed snub. Johnson handled it by ignoring it—really ignoring it, not merely pretending to. He held no "resentment"; he simply waited for de Gaulle to make up his mind between the shadow of pride and protocol and the substance of their joint problems as world statesmen; he never had any doubt that the Frenchman in the end would choose the substance.

The second reason that Johnson rejected early proposals that he turn out all the Kennedy advisers posthaste was, simply, that he values competence and knows it when he sees it. No staff associate has ever worked his way with him simply by being a good, likable fellow. The President turns to men who can deliver the goods when he wants them delivered and especially to those who in one way or another naturally and easily lead and inspire other to get the job done. When he finds such a man, he calls him "a lead horse" or "a stud duck." This is his highest accolade; it means that the President has studied the man in question and has judged him competent to do not merely his own job well but also to cause others to do the same.

He had his lead horses and stud ducks in the Senate; he has them in his administration, notably Secretary of Defense Robert McNamara and Secretary of State Dean Rusk. Of course, a truly top-flight lead horse or stud duck, such as these two, has the President's affection as well as his respect. But affection or not, a lead horse or a stud duck is the sort of man in whom the President is always interested.

6

BEFORE POLITICS

THE LONG ROAD THAT TOOK LYNDON Baines Johnson to the Presidency of the United States opened for him on August 27, 1908 in the dry, unrewarding, undramatic hills of southwest Texas near the crossroads hamlet of Hye, near the small village of Stonewall and the slightly larger old frontier post of Johnson City. It was, and is, "little ranch" country. The great, lush spreads to be found farther south in Texas, near where the grass line runs down to the Gulf of Mexico, are not to be found around Johnson City.

It is a poor, but not crabbed, kind of country. (In Texas any given area or type of soil is often called "a country" and not simply a neighborhood or region.) It is a bleak, but not mean, country; Spartan but never Puritan, as is a good deal of Texas to the north and west. It is a country populated by the descendants of the English and Scottish, most of whom came in from the deep South after the Civil War. There is also a very heavy leavening of German-Americans, especially in and about the area's metropolitan town of Fredericksburg. It is a country that has Catholic and Lutheran churches as well as that ecclesiastical triad that exclusively ministers for God in many small Texas towns, Baptist, Methodist, and Christian.

Nominally, it is a southern country; but most of all it is simply Texas. In Virginia "the War" to many is, however oddly, still Mister Jefferson's and General Washington's War of the Revolution, not as is often assumed, the Civil War. In the environs of Johnson City, Texas, "the War," so far as legend and romance go, is the War of Liberation from Mexico, which created the Republic of Texas in 1836. To be sure, the erect old horseman who set out on this August Sunday of Lyndon Johnson's birth to call solemnly upon his neighbors and to announce to each "A United States senator was born this morning—my grandson" had himself fought for the South all through the Civil War. But Samuel Ealy Johnson, the founder of Johnson City, had, like combat soldiers after all of history's wars, elected largely to forget the past and to put his face to the future. He carried little of the scent of magnolia in his heart. His wife, Eliza Bunton, was the niece of John Wheeler Bunton, a signer of the Texas Declaration of Independence and of the Constitution of the Republic of Texas.

While Grandfather Sam Ealy Johnson was moving decorously about the community with news that his grandson would be, in due course, on the way to Washington, the child's father, Sam Ealy Johnson, Jr., was already in politics up to his eyes, as a member of the state legislature. He was also under the genial but powerful pressure of his wife, Rebekah Baines, for self-improvement. Rebekah Baines Johnson herself, having worked her way through college after her father had suffered financial setback, had "taught expression" before her marriage. In those dusty days, a young lady who taught expression was herself more or less in politics, for expression, in Texas, anyway, was then one long exercise in debate and declamation over the history and political issues of this country.

Rebekah's father, Joseph Wilson Baines, was, to complete the circle of total political omen and aura which surrounded the infant Lyndon Johnson, himself a member of the legislature, at one time Secretary of State of Texas, and also a schoolteacher and lawyer. And *his* father, George W. Baines, in addition to having published the first Baptist newspaper in Texas as a friend of General Sam Houston, the Liberator, had once served in the legislature of Arkansas.

Into all this oddly complete nexus of family political interest, political service and political savvy, Lyndon Baines Johnson was born in a back-country way and at a backwater sort of time in the progress of this nation. The great oil boom of the twenties had not yet come significantly to Texas. Cattle raising then, far more even than now, was a desperately risky business, for the markets were distant and the nearest railhead was a very long cattle drive away.

Farming in this Johnson City country was not worth a damn, as the expression would have been, for the land was poor, dotted with mesquite and stunted live oak over which buzzards circled lazily in the wide summer sky before plunging upon the carcass of an occasional dead steer. Water was, always and everywhere, a great problem—now a national problem, which rarely leaves the mind of President Lyndon Johnson.

Electric power was something for other people; people in the cities. Flood control and all that was strictly visionary; the Pedernales River, which ran through Grandfather Sam Ealy Johnson's old home-place ranch, was a trickle in dry seasons and a sudden, spurting torrent when rainfall backed up sometimes in the surrounding hills. Either way, there was never the right amount of water; the Pedernales, for lack of control and conservation, was always too low or too high. The fact that it now passes a dam and spillway through the front yard of the old Johnson ranchhouse (now enlarged, modernized and fitted with every creature comfort, not excluding heated swimming pool and piped-in music) is not an accident. Lyndon Johnson long ago tamed, recaptured and held fast the river which in his youth had been so fickle, so wanton, so ill-serving of his struggling kin.

In his boyhood, there was deprivation; there was, by today's affluent standards, something approaching poverty. But at that place and time in Texas (and Texas is as large, complicated, and paradoxical, sometimes, as is the personality of the thirty-sixth President of the United States), it did not seem poverty to Lyndon Johnson. It was only the ordinary course of things; a boy learned early that his way in life would be the way he himself made; there was then no "permissiveness," either in education or in life, for the young.

But if opportunity for higher education, for good jobs, for what is now called social security was very thin, there was also a richness of life for a boy, then, in this sunparched small corner of southwest Texas. This was a time and place of an extraordinary freedom of thought, of argument, discourse, dissent. William Jennings Bryan's modified populism set the theme for many a youthful dialogue. Boys grew up very early. They considered themselves men at sixteen, and, curiously enough, for the most part they behaved accordingly. The debates of United States senators, in faraway Washington, were then somehow more carefully read, more eagerly discussed, than now, for all our vaunted improvement of communication.

Materially, then, life was hard along the Pedernales, and indeed everywhere else in Texas, but it was a fallow and fertile time for the life of the mind. Freedom, a fierce, independent, profound, personal type of freedom, in speech, in attitude, in politics, in religion, in everything, was a powerful, pervasive force in this state over which six flags had flown—the royal standards of Spain and France and Mexico, the single star of the Republic of Texas, then the Stars and Bars of the Confederacy and now, the Stars and Stripes of the United States of America.

It had been an imperial lodgment in the New World. It had been a lonely, solitary outpost of adventurers and dreamers, like Jim Bowie or Stephen F. Austin in the brief, urgent days of the Republic of Texas. It had fought on the side of the Confederacy, although the old Johnson family friend, Sam Houston, had opposed secession to the end and, sometimes, had sat in public meetings with a drawn pistol to see to it that fellow Texans opposing the Confederacy had their chance for free comment and dissent. It had been, then, a part of the South, not really in defense of slavery, which was neither a peculiar institution nor any other kind of real institution in this old Texas, but only in defense of what a majority of its people believed to be the Constitution of the United States. They thought, in short, that whether secession was wise or not, or right or not, it was allowable under that Constitution.

Nowhere, in all this nation, in all this world, were at

least most of man's inalienable rights—to privacy, to fair trial, to the decent respect of his fellow men—more deeply, more stoutly asserted and defended. For this was a state in which the ancient British political values, free elections, trial by jury, Parliament's rightful supremacy over kings and barons, including industrial barons, were the direct legacies of the dominant Anglo-Texans. But some of the softer Spanish values had also come to endure. Such was the granting of a special place to women, expressed in the community property arrangement by which half of what a man had or earned was unarguably and forever his wife's.

It was also a state in which no man could be dispossessed from his home. The homestead, a house and one hundred sixty acres, could be taken for no debt even to the state itself.

In short, it was, in Lyndon Johnson's early and formative period, a place in which, lacking the distractions of things, boys dwelt endlessly upon the political traditions and legends of their heritage. Any boy in that period could become an expert in the great profession of politics, if he chose. Given Lyndon Johnson's special opportunities in this regard, given the family political interests that habitually surrounded him, one sees in the neighborhood of Johnson City, Texas, the origins of a man who was to become one of the master professional politicians of his generation. Given the general circumstances—the presence of competing religions, existing side by side in peace, and the multi-national origins of the people—one sees the roots of Lyndon Johnson's lifelong tolerance.

While he was yet a pre-adolescent, to use a term surely

never even heard of then in Johnson City, his father, Sam
Ealy Johnson, Jr., was deeply troubled at the super-heated
super-"patriotism" aroused among the unthinking against
people of German descent when we entered the First
World War. Sam Johnson as a member of the Texas legislature made a memorable address in Austin denouncing
the persecution of men simply for having German-sound-
ing names, and he took the lead in a moving legislative
demonstration against such excesses. Again, before
Lyndon Johnson had reached the voting age, the Governor of Texas was James E. Ferguson, a bad old boy in some
ways, notably in his indiscreet handling of public funds,
but an indispensable old boy, indeed, in other ways. In
the twenties, Governor Ferguson, with the help of Sam
Ealy Johnson, Jr. and others like him, caused Texas to be
the first state in the Union to bring the Ku Klux Klan law-
fully to its knees by a tough statute making it a crime to
parade and otherwise to operate in masks.

Lyndon Johnson thus learned to fear and to fight bigotry and the lynch spirit before he had learned much
from his books in elementary school.

He was born in what is really one of five Texases, a circumstance that led to a lifetime of misinterpretation by
people who did not know then, and often do not know now,
that Johnson's Texas was never the same as any of the
other four Texases.

There is a brisk northern Texas, running roughly from
Dallas to Amarillo in the Panhandle, which is hardly more
southern than, say, Kansas, but which, for tradition's sake
and for the sport of the thing, on some occasions sentimentally identifies itself with all the other Texases.

There is a sleepy, rich-black loam, east Texas, where life is not dissimilar to that in the Mississippi Delta, and where there is, because of cotton and its consequential heavy population of Negro field hands, an immensely difficult racial problem. Here lives on whatever survives in Texas of the Old Confederacy.

There is a west Texas, beginning about at Forth Worth and running on out to El Paso, occasionally merging here and there with a bit of the terrain and culture of north Texas, which is still a kind of Marshal Dillon state where old Judge Roy Bean used to be the only law west of the Pecos river and where an authentic six-shooter fight around a corral at dusk is still not altogether an unheard of thing. This is the Texas that comes nearest, in a relative sense, to justifying the long, turgid labor of Hollywood in the field of the western.

There is a south Texas, with Corpus Christi and Galveston its most charming centers, and Houston, Beaumont and Port Arthur its lusty and urgent and far larger appendages. This is a Texas of giant basic industry, chemicals, steel, oil, shipping, not too unlike the seaport and manufacturing environs of New York—Jersey City, Newark, Hoboken and all the rest—except for differences in regional language and for the ever lessening differences in cultural background, as the old three-fourths southern, one-fourth western culture slowly dies out under northern immigration.

And there is, finally, the southwest Texas of Lyndon Johnson. This is physically not far from the mannered Spanish-laden charm of one of the most beautiful of all American cities, San Antonio, or from the cultivation and curious serenity of Austin, the capital of the state and, more important culturally, the seat of the University of Texas. This university was the very first creation of those old revolutionaries like Houston and Crocket and Stephen Austin and Mirabeau Lamar—and some of Lyndon Johnson's own "connections"—once they had got free of Mexico. They put aside a large stretch of the land wealth of the new Republic for the establishment "of a University of the first rank."

Yet, while Johnson's southwest Texas is not geographically far from Austin or San Antonio, it is still, despite superhighways and all, a world apart.

In a human sense it remains to this day a long way from all the other Texases, a strongly persisting instance of an odd, fractional regionalism within the larger regionalism which is Texas as a whole. In Lyndon Johnson's boyhood, nobody in this "country" was rich, and there were, quite simply and literally, no social classes. The Germans of Fredericksburg, the descendants of men and women who had fled from Prussian Germany in mid-nineteenth century, ran their own show in their own way. They were respectful and friendly toward the Anglos, the predominant population of Johnson City, largely descendants of deep South refugees from Reconstruction. But the intimate affairs of the Germans—birth, marriage, religion, death—they kept to themselves. They also kept, as to this day they keep, their basic loyalty to the Republican Party, perhaps because of its fiscal prudence, perhaps because of its historic association with the preservation of the Union.

The non-Germans, the Johnson City Texans, one might say for convenience, also largely kept to themselves, and within their own group made no social distinctions. Lyndon Johnson was "well connected," in the family sense, but his playmates often lacked any "connection" at all. Johnson was a tall, stringy boy with very black hair, slicked back with the most painful and glistening precision in an era when we all put a substance called "Stacomb" on our hair. From the beginning he was a threshing, human dynamo, endlessly curious, but also endlessly realistic.

His mother, Rebekah Baines Johnson, once recalled that when he was very young she read to him stories from history, mythology and the Holy Bible. He liked them, she said, but when she would come to the end of each of them he would demand of her: "Is it true? Did it really happen, Mama?" Still, setting off at the age of five to a country school, he was a far from promising pupil. Though he had learned the alphabet at the age of two, he did not immediately take to learning, as the old phrase went. He was enormously active, and at this period books perhaps seemed to him either "not true" or inert.

His studiousness was not improved by the fact that because he went to school at so early an age—the usual age for beginning school in Texas then was seven—all his friends were older. It was a circumstance that was to endure for most of his life. Wherever he went and whatever he did for many years, he was the youngest.

Imperfect scholar or not, Lyndon was graduated from Johnson City High School in 1924, president of his class and winner of the high school debate contest in the county. At this point, at sixteen, he had reached above six feet in height and was too thin, as they used to say in Johnson City, to throw a shadow at high noon. His mother, whose whole life was spent in encouraging and urging him on, wanted him to go to college. For this, he then had no taste. With five of his friends he formed a go-to-California cadre. Out on the Coast, they all quickly ran out of money and had to separate to find jobs which even then, before the arrival of the Great Depression, were not plentiful.

Johnson himself finally hitchhiked back along the hot, endless highways to Texas and Johnson City. It was a good feeling, this arrival, for Johnson City is as deeply a part of him as Hyde Park was of Franklin Roosevelt. But there was a disturbed feeling, too. In this short, poignant period of rootlessness, of homelessness, of joblessness, Lyndon Johnson for the first time began to feel a horror at human conditions such as these and a deep compassion for their victims. The horror and compassion, he has never, to my knowledge, directly or fully expressed to any living person. He recoils in an almost exaggerated way from anything that could be called the social-worker approach to life's problems, and his strange private reticence, underlying a sometimes gusty and excessive lack of public reticence, makes it difficult for him to use such terms as "horror" and "compassion." This man, profoundly sophisticated as he is below a surface of simplicity, even sometimes of naïveté, is in one sense what he was as a schoolboy. He'll be damned if *he* will ever be known as a "good boy" or a teacher's pet.

The rootless boys with whom he moved and talked on the way to California and back were never forgotten, any more than were the far more rootless boys, numbering not dozens but thousands and tens of thousands, who later became his special charges when he was administrator in Texas for the National Youth Administration, one of those wonderful, sometimes wild things that the Roosevelt administration introduced to this country during the Great Depression. "Wild" things? Yes, there would come a time, many years later, when Johnson himself would concede that perhaps some of the programs of his unrivalled hero, Roosevelt, looked a bit chancy, in restrospect. "But anyhow," he would say, "maybe we had some crackpots in those days. But, by God, you've got to say this: We had no punkin'-heads"—meaning dolts and dullards.

Back from California, in the era in which immense and then uncontrollable economic forces were pushing the country to a dizzying plateau of business-more-than-usual, Johnson cast about for something to do. College still held no enchantment for him; he was a man and in those days men around Johnson City mainly were meant to go to work. He got a job on a road gang, shoveling gravel, pushing a wheelbarrow and then moved up to driving a truck.

On Saturday nights he "went out among 'em," meaning, in the Texas mores of that time, that he got into an old Ford, perhaps with one or two other boys, and went calling on the girls. In the form of the day, these were not *home* girls; one felt obliged by social manliness to go far afield; perhaps even fifteen or twenty miles. They were long miles, then, over bumpy roads lit only by the flickering lamps on the Ford's fenders and the wash of a moon which is, in sober truth, luminous in Texas, be it summer or be it fall. It well may be that occasionally there was a bottle of beer or two in the Ford on those nights; the Germans of Fredericksburg did not hold with some of the new fangled things and so went on making their excellent home brew.

Prohibition, that is to say, never came to Fredericksburg; just as other innovations do not, sometimes, entirely come to the country around Johnson City. After the Second World War had drawn to its close, the then Senator Johnson was sitting one evening on the front veranda of the LBJ ranch house with an old friend, Paul Porter, who had struggled most earnestly conducting the Office of Price Administration, with its ration books and all. To a neighboring rancher who was sitting with them, Johnson introduced Porter and praised his work in price control. Porter asked: "What do *you* think, Mr. Jones, of the OPA?" Mr. Jones reflected a moment and replied with grave courtesy: "I don't rightly know, Mr. Porter; you see, they ain't put it in down here."

Still, Saturday night diversions at length seemed to the young Lyndon Johnson to be a poor return for a hard life working on the highway; and Sam and Rebekah Johnson, delighted at these stirrings in the prodigal son, now renewed their appeals to him to go on to college. He decided it was the thing to do, and once having decided, he went at it full tilt. There was, as always, little money in the Johnson family. The son went to the Johnson City bank and borrowed the staggering sum of seventy-five dollars on his own note.

At Southwest Texas State Teachers College, in San Marcos, freshman Lyndon Johnson got a job as a janitor and, because he did the work faster than anybody had done it before, he shortly also got a job as part-time secretary to the college president. Having been slow in the past about this matter of education, he now turned to it in that spirit of hurry-hurry that characterizes everything in his life that he likes doing. Finding time still heavy on his hands, he also became the college's top debater, its foremost campus politician, and the editor of its newspaper. He never had any intention, once he got started, of wasting four years to take a degree. Even though he had entered college having still to complete three months of pre-college work plus the regular four years of college work, he did the whole thing in three and a half years. And during one of these years he was out of college, teaching a rural school in order to find enough money to go on.

The very same academic life which had once so little appealed to him now began to arouse a kind of glowing, compelling interest he was never to lose; to make him, as a politician, deeply committed to public education, especially for the poor. Though teaching was not to be his ultimate career, as even then he knew it would not be, he went to Houston, where he joined the faculty of a high school to teach public speaking and debate. The school was in one of the city's poorer sections and Johnson's class had many Mexican-Americans. These, though common in the big-ranch country, were not numerous around Johnson City. And in Houston, although there was no overt discrimination against them, they generally fared ill.

In his days in Houston Johnson devoted himself most of all to two pursuits: bringing forward the Mexican-American students with whom he dealt, and making his debating teams "the very best in Texas." Once, when his team had suffered a setback in inter-high school competition, he wept with them; many times, also, he stormed at them to urge them on. He developed there an almost excessive respect for academic excellence that continues to this day. It is a side of his private character of which the large public has never heard. Many years later, when a friend holding a major position in public affairs was offered a deanship in an eastern college, Johnson's instant advice to him was: "Take it, for God's sake; nothing in this world brings a man such satisfaction as to be able to teach the young." This gentle advice, from the powerful and thrusting politician then being widely advertised as the "toughest" majority leader ever to sit in the United States Senate, seemed a bit incongruous to the friend. "But look here," he protested, "this dean's job would pay me less than I make—and, let's face it, it would make me a comparatively anonymous figure for the rest of my life."

"To hell with the money," Johnson replied. "And to hell with the 'anonymity.' It is what *you* ought to do; believe me, I would do it if I had the chance, except for the fact that in the end I am more made for this other thing [politics] and I know it."

If the second of his Houston pursuits, the pursuit *through others* of the dream of academic excellence, made him for life a deep, oddly shy friend of education, the first, his efforts to help a Mexican-American minority, made him for life the special friend and champion of that minority. Nothing he ever did while young spread more bread upon the waters of his coming long political career. Lyndon Johnson, some of whose forebears fought the Mexicans to the death a century before, has for more than thirty years held the massive loyalty of the Mexican-Americans in every political race in which he has been involved. That loyalty was one of the great factors in carrying Texas for the Kennedy-Johnson ticket in 1960.

Johnson's relationship with the Mexicans is one of the strangest in American politics. On his side, he likes the Mexicans, without pretense or patronage; he speaks their language to them in a cheerfully pidgin-Spanish manner, happily throwing grammar and syntax out of court and returning *embrazo* (embrace) for *embrazo* without the slightest self-consciousness. On their side, the Mexicans like Johnson, but most of all they respect and trust him.

They respect him because he has never been stickily sentimental with them; making it quite clear that although he holds them in affection and their native Mexico in his good wishes, his ultimate interests are those of his own country. The Latinos, being human, value the affections of the Yanquis, but they also have a special regard for honest power, candidly employed. They detest authoritarianism; but they respect *authority* unashamedly used, and high influence openly exerted, for one's own honest national causes. Johnson knows, as do all men who have had long experience in dealing with the Latin mind and temperament, that the Latinos in their hearts value sound reforms but recoil from the reformist approach from the North. They like a leader, whether their own or a Yanqui who is *muy hombre*, meaning very much a man. Their long friendship with Johnson has been based quite as much on his being *muy hombre* as on the fact that he has sought to give them a square deal, whether in their adopted state of Texas or in their homeland in Mexico.

It is this complex of mutual, human understanding

which gives some promise, in the long run, that Johnson's Presidency will bring about the most soundly based Pan-American relationships yet seen. His approach is far less doctrinaire than has been any approach from Washington in recent years. His policies for Latin American assistance, while founded on generosity, are not at all short on enlightened American self-interest. He wants to help Latin America; but he has no intention of doing so at the cost of any irreplaceable American interest, including the honest interests of honest American investors. The Mexican-Americans are fully aware of this; and they do not disapprove. For they believe candor—if a candor more stylish and oblique than our own Yankee version of it—to be an indispensable part of *muy hombre*.

They have had reasons to trust Lyndon Johnson. One of his first acts as a young Texas congressman in 1939 was to push through for Austin one of the nation's first accomplished slum-clearance programs. He had some fighting to do with powerful Anglo real estate interests, but the Mexicans, the first beneficiaries of the program, never forgot. Again, as a first-term senator, he got word that a Mexican-American soldier killed in Korea had been denied burial in a so-called Anglo cemetery by the foolish and unauthorized decision of a private undertaker in south Texas. Johnson's political pragmatism is undeniably high, but his sense of outrage and pity can also be very high. He was white with fury at this episode and one who saw him that day recalls also that there were tears in his eyes. Using that famous Johnson "pressure," he telephoned the Pentagon and literally ordered the Army to send an aircraft to Texas to take charge of the soldier's body and bring it to Washington for burial, with full military honors, in Arlington National Cemetery.

This was, of course, an act of decency; but it was something more than this, too. South Texas, the home of the great cattle kings, has always been Johnson territory politically; without it he would never have been in the Senate in the first place. It would have been ungenerous but by no means impossible for him to ignore this small, ugly incident. As a United States senator he held no possible responsibility for the act of a single stupid man in a single remote town in Texas. He could easily have pretended not to see it, as many a more famously "liberal" senator might well have done since the alternative was to outrage local feeling in behalf of a victim without friends or access to the punitive power of publicity. But the man had died in defense of the United States and to Johnson this was enough. It is a fact that in all his life, Johnson never held racial animosity, racial feeling, or religious bigotry. Such attitudes simply do not register with him, though it has required many years for this simple fact to overcome in the public mind the stereotypes and clichés that he was only a "southern" politician.

7

CONGRESSIONAL
SECRETARY

Houston did not long hold Johnson; for though teaching was teaching and a very fine thing, politics was politics, an unexampled compulsion. In a special election of 1931, Richard M. Kleberg, a member of the dynasty owning the vast King Ranch in south Texas, a million and a quarter acres of rich land dotted with thousands of head of cattle and also with some highly productive oil wells, was elected to Congress. He asked Johnson, a member of a far poorer ranching family but still in the Texas way a member of the cattleman's clan within which large transactions can still be made solely on the word of two men, to be his congressional secretary. The choice was not accidental. Johnson had participated in Kleberg's campaign with speechmaking and personal persuasion among the younger voters. He came to Washington, in the best automobile he could buy with the funds at hand, just as the Great Depression and the hammer-blows of another Texan, Speaker John N. Garner, were driving the Republicans from the Presidency for what turned out to be twenty years of unbroken Democratic rule.

Johnson surveyed the scene and knew that this was where he had belonged all along. In common with many, he smelt the coming Democratic victory of 1932; in common with fewer he foresaw that a revolution in American politics and American government was coming, too. The rootless ones of his California adventure and the incomparably greater number of rootless, jobless ones now thronging the streets of every American city and lounging hopelessly about even in Johnson City, Texas, must and would be cared for. This he knew, not so much by intellectual processes as by that gift of politicians, the instinctive awareness of change before it arrives. "A politician who can't *feel* a situation without having diagrams drawn up for him is no kind of politician," he once summed up.

Congressman Richard Kleberg, Johnson's employer, was an old-fashioned, patrician gentleman; brave, kind, compassionate but vague, rather like one's idea of a typical member of the British House of Lords. His congressional district he served honorably, but very soon the really practical work was being done by Lyndon Baines Johnson. Everywhere he went when he first arrived in Washington, Johnson asked endless questions of other congressional secretaries and assistants, of congressmen and senators themselves, of the staffs of legislative committees. The questions were endlessly varied, but they always had the same burden. Who has the power and how is it exercised? No man can ask more questions of more people than President Johnson; no President has ever sought advice from so many different kinds of people, and no President has ever more singly made up his own mind in the end.

This was the Johnson technique then as now—to ask everybody who might be supposed to *know* anything, and then to make his own decision as to where to operate, and

how, in behalf of Kleberg and the congressional district
he represented. Very soon he learned that congressmen
who do not know the Washington bureaucracy do not
know how best to serve their own people. He began the
habit of calling urgently on every bureau where any form
of federal relief—drought relief, unemployment relief, or
whatever—was being made available. Kleberg's office began to run up an extraordinary record in the matter of
taking care of the homefolks.

Lyndon Johnson at the same time began to be known,
to those aware of the inner realities, as a congressional
secretary who was something more—a driving, insistent,
perceptive force on Capitol Hill, for all his youth and his
total lack at that time of the great Capitol Hill asset,
seniority. This was largely his own doing, though he had
not inconsiderable indirect help in the fact that State Representative Sam Ealy Johnson, Jr. had been an old friend
of one of the most powerful men in the House in Washington, Sam Rayburn, who was later to become Speaker.

What Johnson did for Kleberg was to blend audacity
with a passion for serving others along with himself. Completely unterrified from the day he arrived in Washington,
he made himself the gentle Kleberg's protector as well as
secretary. In this, he unhesitatingly challenged any man,
of any stature, who sought to take advantage of his boss.
On one memorable occasion this involved a bald challenge, from the congressional secretary in his twenties, to
the Old Man of the House himself, Speaker Garner.

Johnson learned of an effort, no doubt made in behalf
of Garner by some of his subordinates, to give to the
Speaker control over a good deal of local Texas postoffice

patronage which had been traditionally in the charge of the individual congressmen. Of this plot, Johnson quietly informed a young newspaper reporter friend. The subsequent public disclosure, with high, dramatic headlines in Texas about patronage steals in very high Washington places, indeed, caused Old Cactus Jack to draw back from the venture. For days, he went among fellow Texans with a scowling, half-amused, demand: "Who in the hell is this boy Lyndon Johnson; where the hell did Kleberg get a boy with savvy like that?"

Johnson, told of this, grinned briefly and, having stopped the rustlers at the gates of the corral, restlessly looked around for more ways to make himself useful. Congressional secretaries in that period had formed an organization called the Little Congress whose head was called the Speaker. Customarily, the Speaker was chosen from among the veterans; this tradition did not deter Kleberg's man. Before he had been a year in Washington Johnson offered himself for the speakership. He won the office with a technique not dissimilar to the one he used years later in becoming Democratic leader of the Senate. He did not move openly until he had quietly talked to enough of those who did not normally trouble themselves about the matter.

It was, however, the full coming in 1934 of the Roosevelt New Deal, to lift a phrase from its fondest and ablest interpreter, Arthur Schlesinger, Jr., that put Johnson on the main track to the Presidency. The boyhood discussions about the prairie-liberal democracy of such men as William Jennings Bryan; the long memories of what in the milieu of his early youth had been a steady strain of western populism; the enduring shock of his own perception that suffering in this country was great and was becoming intolerable—all these factors moved Lyndon Johnson to embrace the New Deal with a warm heart but also with a cool head.

Washington, of course, was now thronged with New Dealers of all ranks and grades, running from Franklin Roosevelt, down through the Harold Ickeses and Henry Wallaces to the third and fourth levels of the eager young men, fresh from Harvard and Felix Frankfurter's law classes, with such names as Corcoran (Tommy), Cohen (Ben) and Rowe (James), who were going to make America over. These were all "can-do men," as Johnson describes the restless, audacious, going-forward people that he likes. The "can't-do men," who had always profoundly irritated him, were, as he saw it, deservedly out of power—and not a moment too soon.

When the New Deal arrived, he was ready and waiting for it. In his two years in Washington, through asking ceaseless questions, he had armed himself with the most vital knowledge in politics: the knowledge of where power lay, both in the executive branch and in Congress. And he possessed, as well, the second most vital element: he had powerful friends who had learned to respect the political capacities of this gangling young nobody from Texas—his capacity to go through to the end, for the men and the programs in which he believed. He knew the facts of life in the great city of government as few members of Congress itself really knew it.

He had also accomplished the most positively fateful victory in his life, his engagement and marriage to Claudia

(Lady Bird) Taylor. In the letters of politics it is, of course, the form always to say that So and So's wife has made matchless contributions to his career; that without her he would never . . . and so on and so on. The simple truth is that Claudia Taylor made Lyndon Johnson President of the United States to only a slightly smaller degree than he did so himself.

He met her in a flying trip from Washington to Austin in September of 1934. She had a fresh degree from the University of Texas, to which the social and financial elite of the state had always gone and which Lyndon Johnson, as a boy in Johnson City, had thought quite beyond his own scope.

8

A LADY
AND AN ART

TYPICALLY, JOHNSON, ALWAYS IN A hurry, asked "Bird" for a date three minutes after they had met. She, on her side, was in not quite such a rush, as has been true of her ever since in anything involving her life or his career. A dark, petite girl with a soft accent far more "southern" than Lyndon Johnson's, she was on the way back from Austin to her home in east Texas, and so declined Johnson's first invitation. He, perforce, returned in a dash and flurry to Washington, whence he set out to woo her by telegraph and telephone; heedless of money, of which he had little, breathless, as always, in his determination.

At length, Claudia Taylor, whose nickname of Lady Bird, or Bird, as her husband and friends call her, had put an end to "Claudia," except on her birth certificate, married Lyndon Johnson. She was the daughter of an east Texas landowner, and there was comfortable money in her background. All this was useful, of course, to her husband; what was to be incomparably more useful to him was the quiet, persistent, gentle poise of this young woman. Where Johnson was, and is, a storm of purpose and activity, she is a quiet island of restraint and reflectiveness. Where he is, supremely, an activist, she is calmly thoughtful. She reins him in, sometimes, when he does not know it. She never challenges him frontally, and sometimes she smiles when his enthusiasms seem to run out of control. But what Bird thinks is deeply important to Lyndon Johnson. It always has been.

As the wife of perhaps the most tireless politician of his era, she has been through many campaigns of clamor and exhaustion. But never has the clamor in the least affected her judgment and never has the exhaustion permitted her to relax a personal code as light and self-deprecating as a smile at a garden party and as iron as the most inflexible resolve her husband has ever made. Her code requires her, without exception, to do her full duty to him and to her position in life, in large things and in small, without slackening, without complaint, and with a sense of humor and proportion so airily peeping through as to be lost to all but the most closely observant.

She is, to put the thing as precisely as one can, a southern lady of the kind who moved with incredible graciousness through hardship and grief and loss in the War Between the States to emerge darning and patching the last of the faded dresses with mannered jests at their hopeless dowdiness, but with a resolve to keep the old house going to the end of time. In this spirit she has met Lyndon Johnson's reverses and accompanied his triumphs, staying in the background, but always there.

She is no grande dame or madam chairlady and certainly no professional exemplar of Southern Womanhood. Like many southern ladies, whether in this generation or before, she loves the old South but knows its stains and

faults. She will never desert it, but she will never claim
that it is always right. She will do what she can, as she
has always done, to relieve the wrongs. Her compassion
ignores race; her religious feeling accepts no master-creed
as superior to all others, though her own Episcopalianism
is quietly satisfying to her quiet needs.

For her, life with Lyndon has been a gusty business, indeed. He has never thought anything of working a sixteen-hour day, finishing at midnight or one o'clock in the
morning. Time and money are to be spent, but not foolishly or unproductively, and that is that. Now in the
White House, as in his earlier public life, there is no telling
when dinner will or can be served, for the President eats
when the mood is upon him and only when he has done all
the work he can find to do. Nor is there much telling who
will be at the table when the time comes. The President,
who in his business is all business to a degree impossible
quite to comprehend until you have seen him in action,
likes at mealtime to be surrounded by people and not
problems. Especially he likes old friends around him at
dinner, old friends to chaff and who will chaff back at
him while he beams joyously like some patriarch at a family feast, hunching his wide shoulders over his plate and
darting quick, amused glances up and down the board.

This being so, he *has* old friends to dinner, whenever he
feels like it, in absolute confidence that it will all be easily
arranged and in an absolute, cheerful unawareness, after
thirty years of married life, that his sudden, ad hoc
and ad lib manner of inviting guests isn't just the way
everybody does it. If there is a certain tax upon facilities
or the family larder, he quite literally doesn't know it. And

if, in the White House in particular, there is some slight dislocation of precedent and protocol he doesn't know that either. (All this does not, of course, refer to the pre-arranged, formal dinners of state which he gives when he must, but which do not enchant him.) For thirty years it has been this way: The telephone has rung for Mrs. Johnson—from the office of Representative Johnson, of Senator Johnson, of Vice-President Johnson, of President Johnson, and he has said: "Bird, why don't you call So and So to come to supper?"

She simply smiles, says "Yes, Lyndon," and So and So comes to supper. Supper with the Johnsons, in whatever time and in whatever place, is a hospitable and agreeably challenging experience. The President is a gifted mimic and astringently witty, given the right mood. He pinks men; he never flays them. And with him it is women and children first; in this sense he is very "southern," indeed.

He never lampoons or criticizes a woman in these dinnertable japeries; to him they are all non-combatants. Even when some women's organization presses him very hard over some small and, to him, drearily inconsequential issue, he will accept demands upon his time and strength to a degree he would never tolerate from any equivalent group of men. Once, in a brief but spirited falling-out with an equally proud and rugged friend, the President closed the contest in magnanimity by calling a bilateral meeting in his office over a glass or two of whiskey. (Johnson resists all conformisms even here. He *ought* to drink bourbon and branch water; instead he drinks Scotch, sensibly but with zest.) Once amity had been restored by this small cease-fire, the President looked thoughtfully at his now restored pal, and wistfully demanded: "But what of ——— (the friend's wife). Is she going to forgive me, do you think?"

"Well," said the friend in embarrassed hesitancy, "I don't know. She's pretty mad at you . . . and you know how women are."

"Ah, yes," the President replied with a slow grin. "God, isn't it awful how wives stick up for their husbands? What a perfectly awful thing, the crime of loyalty, eh?" He was, of course, greatly pleased that the wife would be difficult to bring around.

At dinner, he may, with a turn of phrase and a sudden, startling change of voice, and with quick sketches in the air with his large hands, recreate a boy he knew forty years ago in Johnson City. Again, he may summon up with absolute clarity in the air above the table some colleague or antagonist of his Senate days, or of his current days, with life-like mimicry. Any man thus "done" by the President, would, if present, find it impossible not to laugh, or to hold resentment.

Johnson, like nearly all great political professionals, like nearly all true veterans in any sort of human contest, is a powerful, relentless antagonist in the contest, reaching for the jugular vein with a hand infinitely practiced and absolutely determined. But when the contest is over he drops all bellicosity. He does not hate, nor can he readily understand political hatred in others. Malice he regards as a jejune illness or aberration, a "two-bit kind of ugliness" which offends his sense of adulthood far more than his sense of ethics.

When he takes off a man at his table, he stops short of

animus. And if at any moment he should in his enthusiasm for the game unconsciously approach it toward any absent person, Mrs. Johnson, down at the far end of the table, will say: "Now, dahlin'. . . ." He will look up at her and smile, shrug his shoulders and lift his hands.

The President, in short, carries the conversation—indeed, every conversation—at his table. But Mrs. Johnson in her calm way only sits at the foot of this table in the purely geographical sense of that term.

It is this incapacity to hate—the instinct inside which says that the time to stop in political battle is well short of any unforgivable extreme—that is the greatest single attribute, and only unique one, of the truly good English or American politician. No other politics in the world regularly exhibits this instinct not to carry one's attack beyond the point of tolerance and decency, no matter how many votes one has in hand and no matter how few votes the opponent has. It has made Britain the oldest continuing island of ordered freedom in the world and the United States the oldest unbroken democracy. A politician has this capacity, or he does not have it, and that is that.

Johnson has always had the respect, at least, of liberals, moderates, conservatives in both parties simply because he has this instinct, as gossamer as a moonbeam but as real and irreplaceable a fact of political life as the Capitol dome.

Richard Nixon, for one example, almost certainly would be President of the United States today if he had had it. For not all of Nixon's useful and decent record as Vice-President under Eisenhower could save him, in his

1960 contest with Kennedy, from the consequences of that violent thirst for attack and attack and yet more attack which had been manifest in his earlier career.

There is nothing fanciful in all this; there only seems to be. High national politics has an unlisted code no less binding on its practitioners, at the end, than are the canons of the bar on lawyers, or the ethical rubrics in the practice of medicine. One can break this code and win— for a time. But one can never win this way at the last. For American politics is not Balkan politics. The sole proper purpose is to defeat the enemy but never to disgrace and destroy him; to kill him in political terms, yes, but not then to grind up the bones of his body and fling them into some bitter lime-pit of everlasting hatred. Here, the game must be played according to the rules, unwritten and un-mentioned though they are. The true purpose of politics is performance; it is not disparagement and it is not punish-ment or revenge. For there are, after all, two parties in this country and long will be, just as there are many no-tions, many prejudices, many interests, and long will be. Politics is action but it is not civil war. Civil war only comes when this truth is forgotten. Lyndon Baines John-son understands this to perfection.

He did not, of course, create the ultimate doctrine of American government, which is the majority's final con-sent to be governed. But as much as any public man in this century he has, without ever formulating his purposes in large, philosophic phrases, exemplified and promoted the moderate way in American public life. To win the game? Yes, by all means. To have his way to the last pos-sible point to which he could have his way? Certainly yes.

But to have his way, and his party's way, *in such a manner as to leave the fewest possible scars and frustrations so that what has at length been agreed upon in strife and struggle may, at last, be operable.*

To proclaim policy is a high presidential function; to *effectuate* policy is a high presidential art. This is Johnson's art. It is an art which I believe, after thirty years of observation and reflection (setting entirely aside a quite unashamed personal affection and admiration for Lyndon Johnson), to be embodied in him as in no other President of my lifetime.

The politics of achievement, as distinguished from the politics of debate and demonstration, is not really a thing of labels; it is a thing of developing an effective consensus. Johnson distrusts and dislikes labels, for others and for himself. Some years ago, he attempted to express his approach to his profession in these terms:

I am a free man, an American, a United States Senator, and a Democrat, in that order.

I am also a liberal, a conservative, a Texan, a tax-payer, a rancher, a businessman, a consumer, a parent, a voter, and not as young as I used to be nor as old as I expect to be— and I am all these things in no fixed order.

I am unaware of any descriptive word in the second paragraph which qualifies, modifies, amends, or is related by hyphenation to the terms listed in the first paragraph. In consequence, I am not able—nor even the least interested in trying—to define my political philosophy by the choice of a one word or two word label. This may be against the tide, but, if so, the choice is deliberate.

At the heart of my own beliefs is a rebellion against this

very process of classifying, labeling and filing Americans under headings: Regional, economic, occupational, religious, racial or otherwise. I bridle at the very casualness with which we have come to ask each other, "What is your political philosophy?"

I resent the question most often not because I suspect it of guile and cunning but for its innocence, the innocence that confuses dogma with philosophy and presumes that the answer can be given in a word or two. Our political philosophies, I have found, are the sum of our life's experience. God made no man so simple or his life so sterile that such experience can be summarized in an adjective.

Yet we seem bent today on reducing every man's philosophy to a mere vital statistic, to the next question asked—of professors, students, public officials, job applicants, business executives, labor leaders and many more—after age, weight, height and color of eyes and hair.

Inquiries of men's philosophies do not fit this context.

It is a part of my own philosophy to regard individuality of political philosophy as a cornerstone of American freedom and, more specifically, as a right expressly implied in our nation's basic law and indispensable to the proper functioning of our system.

Our basic law—the Constitution—is distinctive among the basic law of all nations, even the free nations of the west, in that it prescribes no national dogma: Economic, social or religious.

Free enterprise, for example, is not mentioned. Nor are our parties or the party system. Nor is there any provision to require allegiance to any dogma or doctrine.

Yet government is an expression of philosophy, and active governments are inevitably guided by philosophers. As I see it, the mandate of our system—and, perhaps, the ultimate genius of it—is that the American people should be the true philosophers of the American government within the limits upon governmental powers set by our Constitution.

This is an ennobling concept, yet like many things noble and beautiful it has certain frailties and we seem quick now to crush it. We crush out the individuality of our political beliefs and, by this process of high speed sorting and classifying of Americans, automate our choice of courses and sterilize our explorations of the reasons why.

Some might suggest that my rebellion against this process is a show of the provincial Texan in me. I would disagree. Texans are independent and individual, but not the monopolists of these virtues that we sometimes suppose ourselves to be.

The traits are American in origin and, fortunately for the Republic, are deposited quite widely, not part of certain regional hoards. Thus, I believe it is the American in me—even more than the Texan—that now reacts so strongly against the merging of the individual American into the mass in the name of dogma.

I realize, as I say this, that others might point to the Senate where I serve—and where I am, in fact, a designated leader of the majority party—and suggest that the example there of a two party, two philosophy system contradicts or is in conflict with this thesis. The opposite is so. Had I not been privileged to serve in Congress, I might never have come to hold the respect for individuality of philosophy that I do.

The very purpose of Congress is to arrive at national decisions by bringing together some 531 individuals, representing 170 million individuals, to achieve a consent on the way the nation should go. Were we bound by rigid dogmas, whatever their name, there would be no more cause for assembling Congress than for bringing the Soviet presidium together. We are not so bound, and it is part—a great part—of my own

philosophy that the Congress reaches a very dubious decision
when its choices are made solely by head counts of the partisan
division.

This leads to a listing of the tenets of my own beliefs, the
specific tenets of my own philosophy. I would set them down
this way:

First, I believe every American has something to say and,
under our system, a right to an audience.

Second, I believe there is always a national answer to each
national problem, and, believing this, I do not believe that
there are necessarily two sides to every question.

Third, I regard achievement of the full potential of our resources—physical, human and otherwise—to be the highest
purpose of governmental policies next to the protection of
those rights we regard as inalienable.

Fourth, I regard waste as the continuing enemy of our
society and the prevention of waste—waste of resources, waste
of lives or waste of opportunity—to be one of the most dynamic
of the responsibilities of our government.

These tenets, I concede, are simple. They are certainly personal. For these are not tenets I have embraced or adopted,
but, rather, beliefs I have—over 50 years—developed and
come to follow from my own experience.

In the instance of the first listed, I realize that—in these
times—the notion that each American has something to say
and the right to an audience may seem excessively idealistic.
I do not believe that is so, either in principle or in practice.

I am reminded always in my work at Washington of my own
origins. I was born to the hill country of Texas, a remote region
then, still remote today although less so. My neighbors, friends
and relatives there live independently, self-contained if not
self-sufficient.

They are distant from many national issues, yet neither their
distance nor their limited information on any given subject

makes them any less a party to the national decisions we reach in the halls of Congress. Knowing the folks at Johnson City and Blanco and Stonewall and Hye as I do, I know that it would be much more difficult for me to secure a unanimous agreement among them than among the senators in Washington. Yet, in this individuality, my neighbors—or the constituency of all of Texas—are not different from Americans everywhere. There is likely to be merit in the views of the minority, quite as much as there is wisdom in the views of the majority—which however wise, is never the sum of all wisdom.

What we do too often now is oblige our patience with expedients. To grant audiences to 170 million Americans would be exhausting. So we make our divisions, our classifications and our cross classifications which permit us to forego the listening and the searching we ought to do. Trouble compounds when, having made our divisions on one basis, we extend the application to other issues and other decisions. Here we adopt in our American political philosophy the pattern not of philosophy but of cults devoted to dogma, and we construct false equations which produce false answers.

This equation process is much a part of our party systems, and contributes to the myth of the concept that "there are two sides to every question." True, there are two parties. That is not the same as two sides. But, by maintaining the two side concept we satisfy our conscience—again as a matter of convenience—that when a partisan majority has prevailed there is no need to examine either the majority's side or the minority's side again.

Our reasoning is that since there are two sides, either side would have been acceptable, and hence the answer decided by political strength does not require closer scrutiny.

I think otherwise. This popular view is, I feel, very much counter to our American philosophy based on the thinking of men like Jefferson and Madison. I do not believe we have arrived at an answer until we have found the national answer, the answer all reasonable men can agree upon, and our work is not done until that answer is found—even if the process requires years of our lives.

Here fits the third tenet of my philosophy—and the fourth. Had America been bound by the constitutional convention to the philosophies of the 18th century—and by the limits of the wisdom and vision of those times—we would not have the nation that is ours today. Our rising greatness through more than 180 years has come from our freedom to apply our accumulating knowledge to the processes of our self-government.

Or, to state it another way, this has come because America's course has been left to the living. Thus, the 18th century philosophy of our Constitution has allowed for growth so that it is still strong, still good for our 20th century.

Our nation, like all nations, is possessed of certain resources—resources of nature, resources of position, and resources of the human mind. Without conquest or aggrandizement, we cannot add to these basics. Thus whatever we are to be we must build from those things at our disposal, and to content ourselves with less than the ultimate potential is to deny our heritage and our duty.

Obviously, having come from a land like Texas, I feel this strongly. Of all endeavors on which I have worked in public life, I am proudest of the accomplishments in developing the lower Colorado River during the 1930's and 1940's. It is not the damming of the stream or the harnessing of the floods in which I take pride, but, rather, in the ending of the waste of the region.

The region—so unproductive and insignificant in capacity in my youth—is now a vital part of the national economy and potential. More important, the wastage of human resources in the whole region has been reduced. New horizons have been opened for the fulfillment of young minds, if by nothing more than the advent of electricity into rural homes. Men and women have been released from the waste of drudgery and toil against the unyielding rock of the Texas hills. This is fulfillment of the true responsibility of government.

Conversely, the elimination of waste of this sort carries with it a continuing obligation for government—at all levels—not to create waste itself by extracting from the people the fruits of their new opportunities through improvident excesses in spending and taxing. This is an increasingly critical area for American government, but one in which we sometimes apply false standards.

Government can waste the people's resources by inertia, quite as much as by vigor. . . .

These tenets are the tenets of my political philosophy.

Some who equate personal philosophies with popular dogmas might enquire, endlessly, as to my "position" on this issue or that issue or some other. Philosophies, as I conceive them at least, are not made of answers to issues, but of approaches more enduring and encompassing than that. By these approaches I have set down I can seek and, I believe, find answers to the issues of 1958 or 1978, as they arise.

By personal choice, I am a Democrat, for I can in that party best apply and express my beliefs.

As for being anything else, the definitions of what I am will have to be applied by others as they see fit, for I make no such distinctions myself.

I am, as I said in the beginning, a free man, an American, a United States senator, and a Democrat, in that order, and there, for me, the classifying stops.

To the President's art, Claudia (Lady Bird) Johnson has greatly contributed. She has not done so by mak-

ing speeches about it, or by attempting to instruct her
restless and proud husband in his duty, but by setting
for him an example, in the smallest things as well as
the largest, of what all this is, finally, about. What it is,
finally, about, of course, is the need to live a life, public
and personal, of true civility. This does not imply "man-
ners" in some lacy way, nor "culture" in some artsy-
craftsy way. This does not mean "intellectualism" in some
precious, hot-house way; nor, necessarily, reading only
Proust and Robert Frost and never looking at the comic
strips. Nor does it mean, for her, a policy of disdain toward the "politicians," crude or not, who have thronged
her husband's life and her own. It means that with grace
and humor—and very great practical political understanding underneath the soft, hesitant manner and the drawling tones of her voice—she has both lived her husband's
life and prevented it from becoming totally drawn in upon
the one practice in all the world that really interests him,
the pursuit of politics as the means to political power, for
himself and for the ideas and interests in which he believes. Without her, Lyndon Johnson would be, and could
be, no less talented; but without her he could well be an
island of undeniable talent surrounded by a large sea of
unawareness of anything much outside of the art and
science of government.

When he was majority leader of the Senate, she never
intruded upon him; but she kept quietly pressing upon
him interests outside that cantankerous body which so
consumed his time and life. When he was Vice-President,
walking a lonely and a difficult road, she accompanied
him on his whirlwind trips abroad, smiling at the discom-

forts and meeting the peoples of the world with the calm, unstudied, unpretentious good will and true concern with which she has met so many people here at home.

The days of the Vice-Presidency, and particularly the earlier ones before her husband had found his useful place in this new scheme of things, were not always easy for her. The best will in the world could not altogether hide the feeling of letdown. A Vice-President's wife largely opens bazaars, talks to Girl Scouts, and entertains such visiting Very Important Persons as are not entertained at the White House itself. A majority leader's wife—particularly the wife of this majority leader—is, inevitably and always, caught up in a much more real, much more stirring, world, both socially and substantially. But Mrs. Johnson took the rough with the smooth, and loyally and faithfully assisted Mrs. Kennedy at every possible opportunity and in every possible way.

She did not function then, as she does not function now, with any great interest in the society pages. There is no will to queenliness in her; her sense of humor and of the true fitness of things is astonishingly robust, issuing as it does from this small, dark, twinklingly demure, highly feminine person. In dress she is casually chic. In conversation she is very quick to the point; in a paradoxically drawling way she speaks a great deal more pungently than, somehow, she seems to speak. One later remembers quiet, off-hand remarks that did not, at the time, especially impinge upon the consciousness. She knows all there is to know about Lyndon Johnson; and notably she knows that the old saying that leading horses to water does not involve a certainty they will drink, is notably applicable to husbands—and most certainly to hers.

9

NEW DEAL
AND WAR

LYNDON JOHNSON'S FOUR YEARS AS secretary, alter-ego, and vital first assistant to Congressman Richard Kleberg transformed him from a boy to a man in far more than the merely chronological sense. These years formed an odd, indeed an unexampled, postgraduate course, for a very apt pupil, in several subjects of a curriculum which instinctively he laid out for himself and which he pursued with dogged persistence. At the end he had extracted the last ounce of knowledge from all its aspects: the identification, pursuit, capture and use of political power in the great public community of Washington—the White House, the Congress, the bureaucracy, the party national committees. The identification, pursuit, capture and mutual use of friendships with low and high; clerical help in Congress; members of Congress; the Roosevelt assistants of that moving and sometimes chaotic New Deal era; and finally a friendship with President Roosevelt himself.

Roosevelt's palace guard had found first to their incredulity, and then to their puzzled delight, that Johnson shared their dreams, often vaguely and rather grandly put, for a "better America." They found that he understood how to define these notions in realism and to bring them to life through a tactile awareness of how things were actually achieved in Congress. They wrote the lyrics of the great reforms of the 'thirties; in some cases he, this thin, intense, colloquially speaking Texan, actually wrote the melodies, though incomparably more well-placed figures on Capitol Hill had their names on the programs of the finished productions. Naturally, they reported back to Roosevelt from time to time about this odd "natural" who had, God knew how, sprung so improbably from the thin brush of southwest Texas—and from a *Teachers College.*

Roosevelt's towering pragmatism permitted him to suffer and make use of high-minded but sometimes impractical professorial advice which in private actively bored him. He discovered to his amused pleasure that in "that boy from Texas" he had run upon a truly kindred spirit. Johnson's compassion, too, was moved by common man; Johnson, too, had a fire in his belly to change much that ought to be changed. But Johnson had more than the pity and the flame. He had that capacity, so rare in the reformist, to comprehend that good intentions could start the job but that only hard, practical political expertise could finish it.

Thus when one of the most successful and basically sound of Mr. Roosevelt's myriad alphabetical agencies of relief and rehabilitation, the National Youth Administration, came out of the minds of the dreamers and ran the gauntlet of congressional approval, with much sub-rosa assistance from a congressional secretary named Johnson, Roosevelt picked Johnson to be one of its pilot-model state administrators. Resigning from Kleberg's service in 1935,

Johnson swept down upon his native Texas in characteristic array. He carried no brief case, no prepared handouts for the press in Austin. On his arrival, he visited upon the long-suffering heads of the waiting public, and also the waiting state politicians in the capitol at Austin, none of the high-flown pedagese-bureaucratese with which much of NYA was shortly to suffuse the bewildered provinces. He carried to Texas only what was in his head, plus the usual Johnsonian determination to make his bailiwick in this project the best in the country, for certain, and the biggest, too, if that could be brought about.

He meant to put young men to work. He meant also to restore their morale and their sense of belonging, usefully and with dignity, to the United States of America and to the national community of performing persons. But he knew his people down there; he had not become administrator of NYA to come down and pour upon them what was still—and to a degree yet remains—the hateful oil of an unctuous federal daddy-knows-best mixture of aid and homily. First, he put tens of thousands of young Texans to work, the made-work of that period: playgrounds, parks, soil-saving projects subsidized by the federal government. But this was only the beginning; he always knew the shortcomings of made-work. And so he set out upon a vehement round of negotiation with private employers to give this boy and that boy a chance, however hard jobs came then, in private and permanent employment. He placed an extraordinarily large number—twelve thousand in the end, and, altogether, he got assistance for eighteen thousand more in finishing high school or college, or both.

In a sense, it was the most satisfying job of his life until he reached the Presidency itself. For here in the NYA were combined, in a small way, those functions which the Presidency now gives him in an infinitely larger way, the functions of a teacher, an administrator and a politician, the most agreeable possible mixture to Johnson's temperament. He could do good without pomposity; he could instruct without sermonizing; he could use the politician's art and the administrator's technique in precisely the blend that suited him most. It was no accident that nearly two decades later one of his early acts as President was to open his "war on poverty" with an effort at youthful rescue and rehabilitation through education and job training as the core of the program.

In the meantime, the NYA experience in Texas was another block in that mosaic of political support that would one day send him on to higher things. Thirty thousand remembering and grateful young people, impressed for life with what "Lyn" had done for them and to them, formed the human base from which shortly he was to emerge as an elected politician, forever leaving his old role as an unchosen politician in the service of others who had been chosen. The opportunity came in 1937 with the death of the aristocratic Representative James P. Buchanan, a veteran congressman from the Austin district who had looked with a somewhat kindly aloofness at the frantic doings in Washington of the Rooseveltians. It was a world old Mr. Buchanan had never made and which did not find glad response in his traditional heart.

Roosevelt at this moment was trying to pack the United States Supreme Court, which was then looking upon his innovations with far less hospitality than had been shown even by the "Buck" Buchanans of Congress. Johnson was ready; with the right convictions and, equally, or perhaps even more important, with the right professional equipment. He entered a field of ten candidates; this was a special, "sudden-death" election with no preliminaries. The winner would take all. It became the Nine against the One. The Nine were solid men in middle life, well known in the district and generally reflecting a slow but perceptible turn away from the New Deal, a turn now quickened by what was widely seen as Roosevelt's unconstitutional assault upon an independent judiciary.

The One had yet to reach his thirtieth birthday. Moreover, he was scored with the impalpable but very real brand of the outsider. He knew that in upholding Roosevelt on the court-packing plan he was running against deep-seated Texan mores, which tend to hold judges in higher esteem than any other public officials, not excluding Presidents of the United States. But he felt also that Roosevelt had to be supported here; for he himself had assisted in his own way in the enactment of some of the reforms the Court was striking down. But most of all, he simply knew that he had no chance at all—young, untried, inevitably somewhat alien as a politician with ineradicable ties to "Washington"—unless he could force major attention upon himself.

By going all-out for court-packing, he received massive attention, indeed. The Nine in common turned upon him; for here was the sole issue on which all could stand together and from which each thought he could profit without giving affront to the supporters of all the others; supporters who might yet somehow be weaned away. For

Johnson, it was audacity-plus, the precise technique he has all his life adopted, coolly and calmly, when he has only one way to go, that way being up. The Nine denounced him so violently and so much—usurper, traitor to tradition, "Washington man," and all the rest—that soon he was incomparably the best known, if not the most favorably known, of all the ten. Roosevelt himself pitched in; in a flying trip to Texas during the campaign he publicly remarked upon high qualities in the young candidate which even he had not before fully discerned.

Johnson himself campaigned through eighteen-hour days and nights; so did Mrs. Johnson and so did the young generation. The contest was curiously similar, in this respect, to the Kennedy-Johnson presidential campaign twenty-three years later. The coming-up generation was pitted against the generation that was going down. And at the end of it all, Johnson got the news in a hospital bed to which appendicitis had sent him two days before the campaign had closed. He had won decisively. Mrs. Johnson had helped win "the University crowd," the Austin elite whose good will was of more use than their total vote would indicate. Johnson had scored heavily in the surrounding rural ranch-farm counties, in which he had campaigned without apologizing for his locally lamentable Washington connections, and dressed, indeed, in the finest suits he could afford to buy.

He went to the House of Representatives under the brightest of all possible omens. Roosevelt's favor shone through at once, in approving the public power dams with which Johnson was shortly to transform the Colorado River basin in his district, in setting up rural electrification developments in that district which were the first and biggest in the United States. And so on. Hierarchical House favor gleamed at once from the bald, paternal head of Representative Sam Rayburn of Texas, who had just become majority leader of the House, and from Representative Fred Vinson of Kentucky, later to become Chief Justice of the United States.

Now, to be elected to the House is one thing; to be effective there is quite another. Effectiveness arrives only when one has obtained a seat on an important committee; and the custom is to put off the newcomer with an assignment to a committee remote from the great matters of the Republic; concerned instead, say, with the tediously local affairs of the District of Columbia. Johnson had been elected, but he was not really within the lodge. There was, however, Rayburn, who still affectionately remembered his old colleague in the Texas legislature, the father of this stripling member of the national House. There was Fred Vinson, to whom any friend of Rayburn's was, automatically, a cherished person. And there was, most of all, Franklin Delano Roosevelt down in the White House.

President Johnson, in a mood of reminiscence, still occasionally tells the story, with fond nostalgia, of how freshman Congressman Lyndon B. Johnson went onto the powerful Naval Affairs Commitee in his very first days in the House of Representatives. "Mr. Roosevelt," he says with a grin, "had Fred Vinson down to the White House for dinner one night. They talked casually of many things; and Vinson, who knew Roosevelt, kept wondering when the Old Man would say what Vinson was really there for. Finally, after dinner, Roosevelt said, 'Fred, you know that young fellow Lyndon Johnson? It would be a fine thing, I think, if he went onto some important committee—say Naval Affairs. He could be a big help there—to me and to the country.' "

Vinson returned to the Capitol next day with the message firmly in mind. He was a powerful member of the House Committee on Ways and Means, which under one of its hats makes up the list of Democratic committee assignments. To the surprise of few, Johnson's name came out on that list for Naval Affairs. He had reached an inner place in the House the easy way, and he had also opened with Rayburn one of the greatest political relationships of our time. Texans are famous in Washington for standing together; there is a Texan society for mutual protection not unlike that maintained in the Army by West Point officers and in the Navy by old boys from the Academy at Annapolis.

But it was not merely Texas that brought Rayburn and Johnson together and held them together until death struck down the old Speaker in 1962 at the end of the longest and one of the greatest careers in the history of the House of Representatives. What most of all cemented them was a common view of what they both held to be the highest mission and ideal of American politics: a true and final cease-fire between North and South so that while Appomattox would still be remembered for its gallantry and tragedy, this would be in truth one nation with every sectional political scar healed and every lingering bitterness washed away.

They wanted an end to sectionalism, first within their own Democratic Party and then within the nation. And

to this high design they gave, always, an unexampled measure of devotion and an unexampled measure of practical
skill in operation. All this at length permitted two Texans
to control not only a whole series of Congresses, with Rayburn as Speaker of the House and Johnson as majority
leader of the Senate, but also for a long time to influence
the whole course of the Democratic Party as no other two
men outside the White House had ever done. Not since
the Civil War had southern leadership been so powerful
in Congress; never had southern leadership in Congress
worked so tirelessly and so powerfully to bring the South
fully back into the Union. They understood their section's
traditional values and virtues; and these they defended.
But equally they understood its traditional shortcomings
and ancient prejudices, and these they slowly but tirelessly fought with the most subtle of weapons, and finally
with success. Always they refused to range their vast
power in Congress on the side of unreasonable southern
demands; never would they permit counter-demands from
the North to become punitive instead of merely just.

In the eight years of the Republican Presidency of
Dwight Eisenhower, they met him as great political professionals will always meet an adversary. They granted
him all his rights as President but they made it abundantly
and repeatedly clear to him that while a Republican mandate undeniably extended over the White House, a Democratic mandate no less undeniably extended over the Congress. And they ran the congressional show with an expertise with which he never, in simple fact, was able to
run the Presidency. They led him more than he led them;
but they did it with unbroken civility, and more than once

they pulled him from some political ditch when his lack of political understanding had caused him to lose his footing. A mere Republican named Eisenhower they were quite willing to see brought down; a President of the United States named Eisenhower, they would never humiliate. Nor did they ever permit their more zealously and crudely partisan Democratic followers to do so.

It was an extraordinary manifestation, this eight-year period, of a large-minded generosity on both sides plus a very high degree of adult political skill on the congressional side. It was also a manifestation of the extraordinary capacity of the American system of government to operate in full faithfulness to the Constitutional division of powers, as between executive and legislative, without falling into sterile, destructive and paralyzing quarrels between the two centers of power.

As the masters of Congress, they denied Eisenhower everything he sought which would have tended to repudiate any of the twenty Democratic years in the White House that had gone before him. All the reforms of the past they protected and some, indeed, they enlarged, sometimes with the President's consent, sometimes only with his reluctant acquiescence to the realities of the power balance. But they refused, always, simply to "bite at him"—in Johnson's phrase—and notably they refused to do so in matters of foreign policy. They did not believe in, they did not tolerate, partisanship for its own sake.

An article of old Rayburn's faith was that in foreign affairs there could be only one President at a time. This, too, was Johnson's faith. He did not learn it as a pupil learns from a teacher; it had been a part of him from the time when as a boy in Johnson City he had discussed the Presidency with his teachers, with his father's political friends, with all who would show an interest in public affairs.

Johnson as a young congressman fell under Rayburn's approving eye, in short, for several reasons, of which the most profound was Rayburn's recognition that these two, so different in so many ways, were basically alike in public philosophy. There was, in a way, a father-son relationship; but never one of master and servant. Johnson, tall, everlastingly restless, was a "go-along man" but he was also, as Rayburn once said to a mutual friend, "a damn' independent boy; independent as a hog on ice." Rayburn, short, compact, had a far less urgent personality; and at times he deplored Johnson's need to be always in a great hurry about everything to which he put his hand.

So, they disagreed at times, as at other times they mildly differed. But never on any issue, whether involving Democratic Party politics or legislation, did any disagreement persist. It could not, in fact. For Johnson's famous power of persuasion was successful with Rayburn, too, whenever it had to be.

The Speaker, for one illustration, was at first deeply unhappy when Johnson in 1960 agreed to accept second place on the Democratic national ticket. He regarded Johnson as the superior candidate, an estimate undoubtedly not entirely free of human affection and human bias. And he feared a divisive effect in the country from the power of that mighty gathering of urban Democratic leaders and bosses who had made Kennedy's nomination possible. Still when Johnson had talked to him fully, Rayburn went along, somewhat grumpily at first, but then in good heart, as he reflected upon his old protégé's reasons for accepting—to keep the party together and to give it a good chance in November.

This was one of the Speaker's last services to his friend; for he returned to Congress from the election of 1960 with only months of life left. As he lay dying of cancer in a hospital in Dallas, the most broken of his farewell callers was Lyndon B. Johnson. Johnson emerged from the sick room in the grip of grief that has not yet fully left him and perhaps never will. One night in the library of The Elms, while he was still waiting to move into the White House as the new President, he stood a long moment before Rayburn's portrait, hanging alone on one wall, and said softly to the old Speaker's painted features: "God! how I wish you were here with me now!"

Though Rayburn could no longer be with him, he left a rich legacy to the now middle-aged President of the United States in having introduced him, with such high credentials so long ago, to the inner society of Congress in the House. For Johnson took to the life of the House as though it had been pre-designed for him, the way having been smoothed in advance.

In the early years there, his principal legislative chief was the famous Representative Carl Vinson of Georgia (no relation to the equally puissant Fred Vinson of Kentucky). Carl Winson was chairman of the House Naval Affairs Committee, which was later to be merged with the Military Affairs (Army) Committee into a large and vastly influential complex called the Committee on the

Armed Services. And these were the years when the old blue-water President, Franklin D. Roosevelt, was with a sort of calm passion building up the United States Navy as the first move in a long, untrumpeted plan to bring this nation to fighting trim for what he knew to be an inevitable and mortal contest with Hitlerism.

Lyndon Johnson became, and remains to this day, a Big Navy man—and also a Big Army, Big Air Force, Big Marine Corps man. All this, too, was congenial to his personality, his background and all his circumstances, including the fact that he had sworn a private oath of loyalty to Franklin Roosevelt as his greatest public hero in all our history. Indeed he has kept that loyalty to this day. One has a curious collateral recollection, parenthetically, that *Rayburn's* greatest hero was General Robert E. Lee, a photograph of whom, mounted on his horse, Traveler, hung upon the wall of the Speaker's most private, and favorite, office. To Rayburn the past was always powerful; to Johnson the past was, and is, for the most part, simply the past.

Texas is a martial State. They raise their share of foolish men there, but the density of pacifists and neutralists and conscientious objectors is as thin as the density of cloud over Johnson City on a hot day in July. Texas was, and is, full of military installations which were not established there wholly by chance but very often because of casually demanding interventions in Washington by Lyndon Baines Johnson. Moreover, Johnson's own family history has been full of men at arms, not professionals, but citizen-soldiers and sailors whose family habit has been to come forward when the call has sounded.

For all these reasons, Johnson became an eager and apt pupil and part of the genial, decent and important conspiracy, running from the White House to the Carl Vinsons of Congress, which was at length to give this country some kind of armed strength before the great blow fell on Pearl Harbor. Johnson gladly took instruction from "Uncle Carl" in the extremely difficult task of persuading Congress and country that isolationism, both political and military, was rightly dead. It was a hard job, for the forces of splendid isolation, of Anglophobia, of wait-and-see, of neutralism, of a certain pro-Germanism (which was not intentionally pro-Hitlerism), were then very strong in Congress and in the country.

They had to work a hard passage, the Vinsons and their junior associates, and they never could have worked it had they been armed only with good intentions. But they had with them at the onset not a majority of the House but a clear majority of the elite of the House, over which bald, glowering old Rayburn was slowly working his always somewhat imperious will. And they had Roosevelt's rather more cautious, but still devoted, support. For "Uncle Carl," Johnson ran errands large and small as a junior member of a committee in which, even more than in most congressional committees, the seniors believed that the juniors should be seen and not heard. He persuaded, he lobbied, and he spoke loudly and publicly, for a new and true American rearmament against the gathering storm. And, as 1941 neared its end and the terrifying size and configuration of that storm could be seen by those bold enough to drown their dreams in the icy waters of realism, Johnson performed what he still regards as one of the most satisfying acts of his life.

His political antennae were twitching in alarm; he sensed that the mood of the House was turning fatefully against renewing the very foundation stone of any sensible military preparation: the military draft. Young and troubled and keenly aware that he was a second lieutenant going to instruct the commanding general, he went to Rayburn. "We are in trouble, Mr. Speaker; this country is in trouble," he said. "I can feel it so strongly that I can almost touch it. We are about to lose the vote on draft extension." What, then, said the Speaker, did Johnson propose should be done?

"Ask Cordell Hull [then Roosevelt's Secretary of State] to write the House a letter appealing for that draft extension as he never appealed before in his life," replied Johnson. "But, good God, Lyndon," Rayburn replied, half impressed and half impatient, "Hull hasn't got anything directly to do with the draft; that's the military's business."

"Ask him to write the letter anyhow, Mr. Speaker," Johnson pressed his appeal. Rayburn did ask, and Hull did write. And almost on the eve of the Pearl Harbor catastrophe, the House renewed the draft by the margin of a single vote. That roll call separated the men from the boys, and again Johnson emerged as a man. The common run of the House knew nothing of his hand in this affair; but the hierarchs did. And at that moment he entered the comradeship of the untitled, unmentioned club of the powerful and responsible who, at the end, run the House of Representatives.

Why did he ask for a letter from Hull, rather than from

Roosevelt himself or from some official more formally responsible for military preparations? Because already he knew how to gauge the feeling of the House. Because he knew, in this instance, that it was hesitant and fearful of Roosevelt's leadership, seen then as the arch-symbol of American intervention in war. Because he knew that the House wanted the reassurance and the companionship of an old House member in what was supposed to be an adventure in militarism which would affront the country. Hull had long served in the House; the older men all remembered him there; the younger men respected him for it and thought of him, in this critical moment, as one of their own.

Two years before, in 1939, the isolationists, the honest but deluded peace-seekers, the economizers, and those who were habitually anti-Roosevelt in principle or in vengeance for his transgressions upon the rights and feelings of Congress, had all but strangled this nation in the Pacific. By a rider on a Navy appropriations bill they sought to prevent a strengthening of our fortifications on Guam, which was later overrun by the Japanese in that indescribably melancholy phase when Allied positions in the Pacific were falling one by one and it seemed for a time that we should fight at last with our backs to San Francisco and Seattle.

Johnson had helped lead the fight in the House against this profoundly short-sighted measure as he also, in 1941, put all his sharply rising parliamentary skill into the struggle to approve the Lend-Lease program, later described by Winston Churchill as the most unsordid act of high policy in human history.

He was a "War Party" member then; and in an advanced and exposed role, at that. For his Congressional district was a small, imperfect, but real microcosm of the national political divisions of those days. Speaking generally, congressional areas where Americans of British descent dominated were, if not interventionist, at any rate not hostile to assisting the British in "all measures short of war." But men from Congressional areas of substantial German-American influence were, for the most part, walking a cautious road. Although German-Americans were not preponderantly, or even generally, in support of Hitler's Germany, they did, nevertheless, still value Germany as a nation, and they had never been keen on Britain, not having forgotten the First World War and the peace for Germany that followed. And there was substantial German-American voter influence in Johnson's district surrounding Austin; not to the degree that there was, say, in Fredericksburg, but it was an important factor all the same.

It was an ironic turn that the young congressman whose father had defended the German-Americans in the First World War, should take the lead in pushing this nation toward the Allies in the Second World War. But push it he did, to the limit, though he never himself expressed or tolerated in others the easy "patriotism" of those who equated German blood with the bloodiness of Adolf Hitler.

He felt a deep sense of responsibility for the interventionist policies he had without exception urged and supported. When the assault fell upon Pearl Harbor on December 7, 1941, an old friend of Johnson's, then based in

New York, telephoned him in Washington. "What are we going to do now, Lyn?" he asked. "I don't know about you," Johnson replied, "but I know what *I'm* going to do. I'm going into the Navy tomorrow." He did not in fact quite meet this deadline, though he made a pretty good run at it. On December 9, 1941, two days after Pearl Harbor, he became the first member of Congress to volunteer for active service in the armed forces. As a lieutenant commander in the Navy he saw combat in the Pacific. In action around New Guinea he was awarded the Silver Star for gallantry by General Douglas MacArthur, whose subsequent contest with President Harry S. Truman found Johnson standing firmly with the Democratic President.

Johnson put the Silver Star away once it had been awarded and never withdrew it from its place in his private life. Indeed, never in those immediately post-war political campaigns in which most young candidates were leaning heavily on their war records did he refer to his own. Nor did the citation ever appear in his official congressional biography.

He had entered the service at the outset of hostilities because he felt that a man of military capability who had urged the great and terrible adventure of war upon others would be "a damn' poor stick of a fellow" not to run its hazards himself. President Roosevelt did not really want the young congressman to go off to war; he would in fact have been far more useful to the high purposes of the conflict had he stayed in the House. Johnson, however, could not see it that way. Nor did he take off his uniform and return to Congress until Roosevelt, under his authority as commander-in-chief, ordered all members of Congress serving in the armed forces to return to their posts in Washington.

Back in Congress, Johnson, now a real power and influence within the elite group that was primarily responsible in the House for military affairs, became one of the most active congressional backers of a relentless prosecution of the war. He cajoled and pleaded and stormed for more and more ships, planes, and military supplies of all kinds. As chairman of the House subcommittee on manpower use in the Navy, he fought for and won a wiser utilization of naval manpower. When he disagreed with the Navy brass, with whom he had long been on affectionate personal terms, he assaulted them all-out; he became, in short, the great champion and symbol of military preparedness in the House. Wherever American fighting men were on short rations, in ammunition, or equipment, they did not remain short if Johnson could find out about it. Though essentially a pro-labor politician, he was steadfast during these urgent war years, in opposing any labor demands for special privileges. He was, not merely sentimentally but in a highly pragmatic and effective way, a pro-foxhole congressman. His personal policy was simple: whatever helped the war he supported with all his strength; whatever impeded it he fought doggedly.

On March 19, 1944, the Johnsons' first daughter, Lynda Bird, was born, an event which stirred the deep patriarchal sense of her father, but to which he was not able to give a great deal of his time. Franklin Roosevelt was by this time a very sick man, and Johnson could see, again more by instinct than conscious process, the beginning of the end of an era which will always be to him the greatest in which he took part until he succeeded to the White House. In a sense, indeed, not even the Presidency is more stirring to him. The old years, the New Deal, the Depression, the War, made ineradicable marks upon him at a more impressionable age. And, as with many men of his generation, these old battles stir up the greatest nostalgia of all. For all his outward face of casual gaiety and robust humor, Lyndon Johnson's sense of tragedy is very real and very deep. He has moods of bleak spiritual unease; he is sometimes temperamental and, for brief, untypical moments, glumly withdraws into a private mood.

Now, in these last months of the war—and also of the life of Franklin Roosevelt—there began two significant, if subtle changes in Johnson's outlook. He saw the immediate problems of America to be those of a world maimed by the human loss and suffering of years of war. It became clear to him that "Dr. New Deal," as Roosevelt had once personified his early years in office, was no longer the relevant physician. Nor was the succeeding "Dr. Win-the-War." The reforms, innovations, and warfare of the 'thirties and early 'forties were not now the real issues.

The relief of American want was no longer in question. The banks were no longer closed, but flourishing. The soup lines, too, were finished. Heavy unemployment had become a memory, although still a nightmare to those who had gone through the Depression. No, the new great issues now were the restoration of a broken world and the containment of Soviet power which Johnson (here more a heeder of Winston Churchill's forebodings than of Franklin Roosevelt's happy optimism) now ceaselessly urged as he opposed the dilution of American military power around the globe.

As the war drew to a close, and Roosevelt's death brought in a new leadership, the shortage of British power in the basin of the Mediterranean laid Turkey and ravaged Greece open to chaos and Communist seizure. Johnson now stood on the House floor in powerful support of the Truman Doctrine. In this memorable program, the then new President Truman opened what was to be the first of a long series of efforts to contain the westward movement of Soviet Communism into the power vacuums that lay all across eastern and Balkan Europe, up to the borders of France.

Two immediate domestic problems faced the country, as Lyndon Johnson saw it. One was the threat to this country's basic economy through an inflation brought on by the determined effort of extreme "free enterprise" forces to strike down price controls. The other was the peril to this country's position in the world through the demand that the boys be brought home, at once, from all the great theatres of war. Against national submission to this sentimentalized homesickness, Johnson spoke out.

About price controls, he could do more. In 1946 he voted against cutting them down, as in 1943 he had voted against a move to cripple the Office of Price Administration by striking $43,000,000 from its vital appropriations. In 1944, he had taken the lead in the House against a bill seeking an increase of thirty-five cents a barrel in the price of crude oil which would have meant a bonanza of billions to those very "oil interests" with which Johnson's "image" would so long and tirelessly be associated by his ultra-liberal critics.

To face effectively both immediate issues, the securing of the domestic economy from the raids of inflationists and the maintenance of a strong world position against the inroads of Soviet power, what were the necessities of American statesmanship?

They were not to extend domestic reform and innovation, though what had already been accomplished along these lines must be protected. The greatest need, underlying all others, was for national unity. The country must be drawn closer together so that, with a new spirit, it could confront the massive enigmas of its new world leadership. We had no longer to reclaim merely our own country and renew its sense of social justice; we had now to reclaim a world, and for this task, we needed a nation looking outward upon its responsibilities, not inward upon its material and social satisfactions.

Johnson was the first of the Roosevelt New Deal politicians fully to understand that the years of domestic rescue and reconstruction were finished. The more he understood this, the more he moved his political position toward the moderate center from the moderate left. This was not because he had become "disenchanted" with the New Deal and its spirit, but because he recognized that new political problems required new approaches. His one unchanging political commitment has always been to informed pragmatism; to flexibility; to a stance open enough both to take advantage of change and to exert some creative effect on it. He recognized that the American people had lost their zest for the New Deal. They still valued it, but now sensed that it had largely served its purpose and should give way to some new approach more in tune with new conditions.

Along with many others Johnson now became convinced that in the postwar world the political and statutory position of the American labor movement had climbed from a place of too great weakness to one of too great power; to a capacity to fetter and even injure the national economy. In 1935 he had voted, without a qualm, for the Wagner Act, Labor's "Magna Carta." In 1946, while his career in the House was drawing toward its close, he voted, again without a qualm, for the Taft-Hartley Act—sometimes called, though most unfairly so, "the slave labor bill." The Wagner Act had been intended to redress the balance between the weak position of labor and the dominance of the corporations. But through the years, it had more than redressed the balance. In 1946 it was business and management which stood in clear need of some reasonable relief.

These two votes, for the Wagner Act of 1935 and the Taft-Hartley Act of 1946, represented not a change in Lyndon Johnson but a change in the realities which underlay both statutes.

10

SENATOR AND
MINORITY LEADER

AS HE TOOK THIS COURSE IN THE
House from left of center to just a shade to its left, Johnson's thought was moving in another direction, too.

The House of Representatives was not geared to make
truly effective and original contributions to the solution
of the new world problems. The future seat of American
legislative power in the atomic age lay, instead, in the
Senate with its great influence in foreign policy. Johnson's
awareness of this fact began to make him somewhat restless. He had got along well in the House and was still
moving upward in its governing hierarchy. But the
House is, at bottom, a place for collective action, a collective action which is inherent in its nature and congenial to its iron rules. In the Senate there is room for intuitive individual action.

Johnson began to think of a place in the body more
hospitable to his highly personalized talents as a politician. Despite his success in the House, where team play
was the order of the day and the necessity of the hour,
he had never been a team man at heart; his nature, to
use a football simile, was not that of a faithful, bulky line-
man but of a flashing running back—a star performer.

The House has little room for stars; but the Senate welcomes them and offers the means for them to shine.

So it was that Johnson began seriously to cast about in 1947, the year of the birth of his second daughter, Lucy Baines, for a means to promote himself, as he had failed to do in 1941. That year he had sought a Senate seat left vacant by the death of Senator Morris Sheppard, the father of Prohibition, an experiment upon which Johnson had looked with a cold eye. The campaign had not been a happy experience. Texas then had as governor a classical demogogue, W. Lee O'Daniel, known as "Pappy," who seemed quite untroubled by the state of the world to which Johnson was giving all his attention. While Johnson spoke plainly to the people of Texas of the war that was all but upon them and of their manifest duty to give up petty privileges—labor's to strike, the farmer's to receive higher subsidies, industry's to more and more profits—O'Daniel spoke only the soothing platitudes of the isolationists and promised whole mountain ranges of pie in the sky.

Roosevelt intervened for Johnson, so far as he dared in the light of his unsuccessful efforts three years earlier to defeat some persons and to elect others to the Senate. Johnson announced his senatorial candidacy from the White House steps, an undeniable mistake in terms of political expediency but a striking illustration of his commitment to FDR. The President himself issued this statement:

"First, it is up to the people of Texas to elect the man they want as their Senator; second, everybody knows that I cannot enter a primary election; and, third, to be truthful all I can say is that Lyndon Johnson is a very old, old friend of mine."

What beat Johnson in the subsequent primary is open to endless argument. Some thought it was resentment at Roosevelt's intervention. The more likely explanation is that Johnson himself was so preoccupied with preparing the country for war. At any rate, he ran a creditable race, losing to O'Daniel by only 1,311 votes. There was more than a suspicion of rough stuff, indeed, at some of the ballot boxes, notably in those deeply conservative pockets of Texas where O'Daniel, a far-out conservative, was notably loved. Many thought that Johnson had been victimized by what politicians call "a fast count," and some of his friends wanted him to contest the election. This he shrugged off impatiently. "No, no!" he said. "That's *this* ball game; let's play again some other time."

Thus he had returned to his seat in the House in late June of 1941, still talking military preparedness, still defending Roosevelt to the people of a state which had clearly turned against him in electing O'Daniel, a violent anti-New Dealer.

This experience of 1941 was firmly in his mind when, in 1947 he made the decision to have another try at the Senate. He again entered the contest, and again ran against an ultra-conservative. His opponent, former Governor Coke Stevenson, was the Texas politician of legend, complete with large white hat and sustained by the frenetic loyalty of the Texas right-wing. This time, Johnson campaigned for keeps. Because he had voted for the Taft-Hartley Act, his opponent accomplished the miraculous; he presented *himself* as the true friend of liberalism, so far as union labor was concerned, and Johnson as the tool of reactionary employers.

Here for the first time Johnson discovered that unthink and newspeak (long before George Orwell immortalized these concepts), by which he would be, throughout most of his career, at the same time dangerously liberal and crassly conservative. While his ultra-liberal critics in the East were picturing him as in pawn to "Texas oil," the Texas oil industry was giving the bulk of its great financial support to Coke Stevenson. While Johnson's ultra-conservative critics in Texas were presenting him as a docile stooge for Roosevelt and Truman, the New and Fair Deals; labor was being, to a somewhat alarming extent, sirened away by Coke Stevenson. The theory was that a man who had voted for Taft-Hartley would never do for the sturdy unionists of Texas.

This towering absurdity drove Johnson into a fury of campaigning far surpassing all his furious exertions of the past. It also led him toward the adoption of that somewhat mordantly humorous philosophy of resignation with which, in his later Senate career, he would have to meet unthink and newspeak on a far grander scale. It also caused him to become more and more convinced that a politics of rationalism was not only the sensible man's position but also an indispensable requirement for effective American government.

He leased a helicopter in which to cover the endless vistas of Texas. "A candidate's speeches can get in the papers and they can go out over the radio," he told a campaign staff member, "but the people want to *see* the candidate, too." Characteristically, he chose the helicopter, an advanced vehicle in those days, with a design which went far beyond the mere problem of transport. He was cocking a fist at fate; or, more exactly, at the current mores of a state. He was refusing to offer any apology for being a new and modern-minded politician in an area undergoing a strong revulsion from what it felt was excessive modernity. He did not merely acknowledge his heretical views; he drummed them in, and very hard. This was in part a reversion to the attention-getting techniques he had used when first he ran for the House as a backer of the Roosevelt court-packing policy. His opponents complained that he was "different," did they? Well, then, by God, so he was; and so he would appear to them beyond the possibility of misunderstanding.

But the more fundamental reason for the use of the helicopter, with the break from old tradition that it implied, was simply this: Johnson has never made the mistake of supposing that a campaign's sole purpose, and sole problem, is an election. He has always known that election is only the first step, and rarely the hardest. The hardest step is for a politician, once elected, to be able to move effectively in his job, to represent a constituency which has been put on plain notice of what he is like and what he means to do after he is in office. Being elected is a great and happy thing, but it is a very thin reward if the man elected finds that his constituency feels deceived and defrauded by him. Feeling that way, a constituency can destroy a politician long before it refuses to reelect him.

Thus, he was writing it in the sky that if Texans chose him for the Senate, they would most certainly get no Coke Stevenson.

This senatorial campaign of 1948 was actually one of

the most significant in the country. In the White House, Harry S. Truman, the Democratic heir to the dead Roosevelt, was in the position once attributed to Marshal Foch in the First World War. His left was broken, about to gather about Henry A. Wallace, who seemed to them the only True Believer among the liberals. His right was in sullen mutiny; in the deep South the third-party candidacy of the Dixiecrat, Strom Thurmond, was being prepared. Only Truman's center was left as a combat-worthy force.

In all these melancholy circumstances, to hold Texas was absolutely vital to the President, and Johnson's campaign in the spring and summer undoubtedly helped materially, if not decisively, to hold it. For in beating Coke Stevenson—as he did, in the thinnest possible way —he also beat down a violent right-wingism among Texas Democrats and so dispersed what had been a gathering threat to Truman's vital center in November.

The Johnson-Coke Stevenson campaign was one of superlatives, even by Texas standards. Stevenson's massive backing needed no rallying; what he had, he simply had and would hold to the end. Johnson, on his side, needed greatly to widen his basic support; for he had yet to win a state-wide race. He hammered day and night at Stevenson's isolationism. He spoke so often, day and night, that toward the end his voice fell to a croak and his body, still thin in those days, shrank so much that his face became a caricature of itself, his eyes seeming to burn from an emaciated countenance, as Booth Mooney has pointed out in *The Lyndon Johnson Story*. The issue came down to this: Could a part of south Texas, the old ranch country, save Johnson? Stevenson himself had big ranching connections; and in the cities and in most of the larger towns he seemed clearly ahead. What rescued Johnson in the end was his old friendship for the Mexican ranch hands and a few of their untypical *patrons,* untypical because they were Johnson men. And even at that, Johnson, at the end of the run-off primary, finished ahead of Coke Stevenson by precisely eighty-seven votes out of nearly 900,000 cast. For a time, jesting colleagues called the new senator "Landslide Lyndon."

Johnson did not enjoy these japes; his sense of humor was a bit bruised, at the moment, and he was positively in no gay, laughing mood. Nor was he for a moment inactive, from that time forward, in taking steps to see to it that he never again would have so close a call. He was so successful in these steps, indeed, that in 1954 he was re-elected by a margin of three to one.

In the meantime, the hairbreadth victory of 1948 left some scars in Texas. Both sides had played for keeps; and in some cases the southern Texas counties which saved Johnson came in with staggering majorities on the order of a hundred to one. The reason was this. In these critical counties Johnson this time had the support of some of the Anglo *patrons* as well as the undeviating loyalty of their Mexican-American *vaqueros* and other employees. It was suggested that this was a boss-led vote; and to a degree it undoubtedly was—although there were plenty of boss-led Stevenson votes, too. The point, however, was that the Mexican-Americans did not in this instance need to be led. Johnson, the *muy hombre,* was *sympatico* to them, always had been, and always would be.

Suits by the Stevenson people to invalidate the election results were followed by successful countersuits by the Johnson people. In these, the old New Deal lawyer friend, Abe Fortas, was a brilliant counsel to LBJ. When, fifteen years later, Johnson became President of the United States, one of the first men welcomed into his new home was Abe Fortas. If Johnson's memory for outright and implacable enemies is long, though rarely vindictive, his memory of friends is longer; and never needs refreshing.

Now, at last, he had found his true place, a place that might have been made with him in mind, so perfectly, so immediately, and with such gusto did he settle into it. He was eminently prepared for the United States Senate. The Senate was eminently prepared to be hospitable to him. He had been known favorably there, if in the rather remote way that the Senate knows the principal, or doing, figures of the House of Representatives. And he was seen in the Senate as the protege of the great Rayburn, the only man in the recent history of the House who could, if quite unconsciously, patronize even the Senate, a body whose capacity for a quiet upmanship over every other branch and forum of the government is remarkably strong.

There is a tradition in the Senate that freshmen members should be seen and not heard, but there are exceptions to this and, indeed to every other senatorial rule and custom, when that body likes and respects a newcomer, and when he has the right kind of friends in the right places. Johnson arrived as a freshman only in the most technical sense. His work on military legislation in the

House had been widely known in the upper body. His long and faithful association with Franklin D. Roosevelt had been well noted. It greatly assisted him with the moderate and liberal Democrats and it did him not the slightest harm even with the crusty old conservative Democrats who had broken many years before with Roosevelt and were currently far from enchanted with President Truman. These accepted the new senator, his deplorable quotient of liberalism notwithstanding, because they respected the quality of his loyalty to a wing of the party which did not appeal personally to them; because of the power and persistence shown in his recent campaign in Texas; because they knew a good parliamentary man when they saw one; and because of his "connections" in and with the South.

There was at that time rising in the Senate a great concern among the more moderate southerners for the future of the Democratic Party as a national institution. They had on the whole stood with Roosevelt—and certainly they had so stood in his relief, agricultural, public power and public housing policies—though they had not been able to accommodate themselves and their political necessities at home to what he had tried to do in the field of civil rights for Negroes. They did not like the mood of rebellion from *all* liberalism which was then growing so patently in the South, nor the rise of third party movements and extreme rightist views. And they did not like the seeming progress being made by the Republicans toward capturing the mind of at least a part of that region.

They saw, in short, that the southern representation in the Senate needed new faces, faces of moderation to resist both the Dixiecrats and the new Republicans in the South. Johnson's was such a face, and his whole record showed that it was an honest face.

Thus, when he entered the Senate, the powers-that-be (and these, then as now, were more the moderate southerners than the conservative southerners) saw to it that he had a first-rate committee assignment. He went onto the Armed Services Committee, the counterpart of the committee on which he had served with distinction in the House, and at once began a renewed career in the field of military preparedness.

He thought President Truman had gone too far in reducing the military establishment in a world where the American nuclear monopoly was now threatened and where international Communism was coldly on the march.

Everywhere he fought for more strength, in the air, on the seas, in the Army, and soon he successfully proposed the establishment of a Senate Preparedness Investigating Subcommittee, of which he was made the head. And though he struggled fiercely against President Truman's military budgets, as too little and too much concerned with the single factor of economy, he stood all the way with the President when he sent troops into Korea in 1950 to establish for all time that the United States, at least, meant what it had said when it had adopted the doctrine of collective security.

When Republicans and dissident Democrats blamed the Korean War on Truman, Johnson retorted: "The Communists, not President Truman, were responsible for the invasion of South Korea. The quicker we direct our hostility to the enemy instead of to our leaders the quicker we will get the job done."

Thus, he became what he had been in the House, the Senate's untitled but acknowledged leader in the area of military preparedness and collective security. All this was made possible in large part by a warm friendship, continuing to this day, with the powerful southern leader, Senator Richard B. Russell of Georgia. Russell was and is chairman of the Armed Services Committee, of which the Preparedness Subcommittee was a part; without Russell's approving nod there never would have been such a subcommittee.

The association between these two became, in fact, one of the most important of all Senate realities. The patrician, fastidious, withdrawn Russell, a few years Johnson's senior and the representative of an old South Johnson never really knew, made an unspoken compact with a man he realized was more liberal and far less southern than himself, but a man he trusted instantly, and still trusts. The two could not agree on many things; but they never disagreed on the great issue of protecting this country by weight of arms so long as weight of arms seemed its only sure salvation. Both followed the dictum of Pascal that force and right must rule this world, and it must be force until the right is ready.

Military preparation, and an increasingly intimate association with foreign policy problems as a necessary corollary of military policy, was not enough for Johnson. As he continued to show a high degree of party and national responsibility, his Senate elders began to talk of him as a potential general party leader. He had the credentials: ability, an unbroken record of faithfulness to his party and its presidential leaders even when that loyalty had been hard on him in the South, a high degree of acceptability to all Democratic factions in the Senate. Thus, as the year 1950 drew to its close it was intimated, in the quiet, oblique way in which the Senate patriarchs do these things, that "Lyndon ought to be considered" for the post of party whip, or assistant floor leader. On January 2, 1951 he was elected whip, at the age of forty-one.

His chief, the Democratic floor leader, was Senator Ernest McFarland of Arizona, an engaging, honorable, and not too effective party spokesman. In the nature of things much of the real burden of leadership fell on Lyndon Johnson, and again he was ready. He loyally supported and loyally deferred to McFarland. Nevertheless, he began to see great gaps in the Democratic line that could be closed by foresight and hard work and by touching all bases among the always fractious and sometimes overly detached individual Democratic members of a highly individualistic body.

Shortly, the party in the Senate took on a new discipline, a new *élan* and, indeed, a new life. Johnson worked to be seen but not heard in public. But no amount of public reticence on his part could hide the fact that improved party effectiveness and morale had not suddenly descended from the brow of some heretofore unkind god of politics.

When Senator McFarland was defeated at home in 1952, the elevation of Johnson to the top place became inevitable. On January 3, 1953, his Democratic colleagues chose him as Democratic floor leader.

He had thought long upon the proper duties of such a leader, and before going into the decisive caucus he told a friend: "I am going to say exactly what I mean in there today. For twenty years I watched the Republicans in Congress act as though they had no function, no mandate, no capacity, to do anything more than constantly bite at Roosevelt and Truman. A party leader who can only say 'no' is no kind of party leader at all, in my book. Twenty years of screaming at Roosevelt and Truman got the Republicans this: the loss of power for twenty years and a reputation in the country for being only nay-sayers. I don't believe that the sole duty of an opposition is just to oppose; I believe the United States Senate has a duty to have its own program, too. Now that the Republicans at last are in the White House, I am not interested in running a party that can *only* attack Eisenhower."

So he entered the caucus and read the following manifesto to his colleagues:

My Democratic colleagues have accorded me the great honor of party floor leadership in the 83rd Congress. I accept the position in a spirit of gratitude for their generous support and with a prayerful hope that I can be worthy of their trust.

I believe that Democrats can all work together in harmony. One of my deepest convictions is that there are more vital issues to hold Democrats together than there are issues to divide them. We have had our differences in the past and will have our differences in the future. I do not believe in suppressing those differences. Unity achieved by muffling dissenting voices is a cheap unity which serves neither our party nor our country.

My voting record is open to all. Regardless of whatever position I may hold in the Democratic Party, I will not change the principles which have guided me in the past nor will I ask any other man to change his principles.

There may be times when I will be in a minority—not just in the Senate but among the Senate Democrats themselves. This I believe is unavoidable and would be unavoidable regardless of any selection that could be made by this conference. No man of integrity can live constantly in the majority.

We have all been sent here by our respective states and we all owe a primary allegiance to our constituents. Since this is a nation made up of states, I have never felt any conflict in loyalty between my state and my nation. I have represented Texas to the best of my ability in the past. I shall continue to do my utmost to safeguard the interests of my native state in the future, and I don't think there is another Senator who will disagree with that thought.

I respect and sympathize with the problems of all of my colleagues. I know they will be generous and extend the same understanding to me.

Wherever possible—and I sincerely believe this will be true in a majority of issues—I will seek to state the position of my colleagues as forcefully and ably as I can. In those instances where we may disagree, I will state and vote my disagreement. But I will do my utmost at the same time to protect the rights of those with whom I disagree.

We must frankly face the fact that the Democratic Party, as well as the nation, is stepping out into new and untried courses. Twenty years of Democratic administrations have come to an end. New issues are arising and new issues will arise which we cannot foresee.

I have a great faith in the Democratic Party. I am a Democrat out of conviction—not out of habit. I believe that the Democratic Party is now—and always has been—the party that is best for America. I believe there are forces holding our party together greater than the issues over which we may squabble for the moment.

We are now in the minority. I have never agreed with the statement that it is "the business of the opposition to oppose." I do not believe the American people have sent us here merely to obstruct.

I believe we are here to fight for a positive program—a program geared NOT just to opposing the majority but to serving America. I think that is the real desire of every Democrat— even though we may disagree as to methods.

Working together, I think we can do more than merely preserve the gains of the past twenty years. I think we can go forward with a positive program—a program that is pro- American and not just anti-Republican. And if we go forward as positive Americans—and not negative oppositionists—I am convinced that the time is not far distant when the Democratic Party will again be in the majority.

Johnson's blunt rejection of a politics of opposition for opposition's sake went down poorly with the more eagerly partisan Democrats, whose resentment at Eisenhower's defeat of Adlai Stevenson had caused them to return to the new Republican-controlled Congress with bitter thoughts of revenge. The campaign understandably had raised the Democratic gorge. The Truman administra- tion had been attacked with rare ferocity as a sort of com- munity sink of "Crime, Communism, Cronyism and Korea." And Stevenson himself had not gone out of his way to defend the outgoing President from some of these violent accusations.

Johnson understood, as Speaker Rayburn also under- stood across the Capitol in the House, that the problems of Democratic leadership would be wholly different from what they had been for a whole political generation, the twenty years of Democratic rule of the White House. A savage emotionalism had, in fact, since 1949 largely ruled the politics of the long-frustrated erstwhile Republican opposition, though Eisenhower himself in the 1952 elections had stood above the battle, campaigning more truly as a coalition leader than as a Republican.

Now, the angry Republicans, who for two decades had not seen the inside of the White House and who had felt a strongly vengeful spirit of their own, were suddenly in control both of White House and of Congress. In the election they had heavily breached the South, not excluding Johnson's Texas. The party professionals were in no mood to deal gently with what they believed to have been an oppressive Democratic majority which had so long stood over them. Left to themselves, the Democratic rank-and-filers were in no mood to be dealt with gently, if it came to that.

Seeing that there was a genuine danger to effective government unless partisan emotions could be brought under control, and convinced also that mere Democratic naysaying and frantic and purely partisan assaults upon Eisenhower would merely postpone Democratic return to power, Johnson concluded that there was but a single absolute necessity for Democratic leadership. This was to present the party to the public as undeniably "responsible." As Roosevelt had liquidated "Dr. New Deal" for "Dr. Win-the-War," Johnson now set out to liquidate "Dr. Fair Deal" in behalf of "Dr. Responsible." He did not for a moment intend to end the *substance* of either the New or Fair Deals; nor did he ever allow any successful attack upon them. He liquidated no policy; he liquidated a semantic image for another image.

This being his basic strategy, he knew that he must from the outset candidly tell his Senate associates what to expect of him. Again, he wanted no office only to find later that his constituency had not understood his purposes and could claim that it had been deceived. So he laid down the rule, as Rayburn laid it down in the House with rather less success, that the Senate Democratic Party under Johnson would never open fire on Eisenhower without decent cause, no matter how ugly the 1952 campaign 'had been. This deeply suited Eisenhower himself. He had not come to the Presidency as a true partisan, no matter what his own campaign associates had said and thought, and he did not mean his Presidency to be one of innovation or revenge, but rather of a magisterial one.

His undoubted basic purpose was national reunion. So there developed an odd relationship between the man who was now in the formal sense a Republican President and the man who was now in the formal sense only a Democratic Senate leader. Eisenhower actually performed as a *national* President; notwithstanding all his mistakes, he put the partisan and institutional Republicans on a very thin diet. Johnson became not simply the leader of Senate Democrats, but in truth, if not in form, the leader of the Democratic Party in the United States.

For his restraint in his formal role brought him an unexampled power far outside the chamber of the Senate. In the eight years of the Eisenhower tenure, Lyndon Johnson often came very close to running this country. He held a power of veto over all of the President's domestic legislative purposes, and in the end, what Johnson wanted, Eisenhower usually got. And in foreign affairs he was incomparably more powerful than the country ever knew. Though he never served on the Foreign Relations Committee—he could not have done so, given his urgent schedule as the Democratic leader—his voice, inside the Senate, was the ultimate voice in all that body's foreign policy decisions.

From beginning to end he put his vast influence into the service of what Eisenhower's foreign policy really was, a continuation of the bipartisan policies of both Roosevelt and Truman. When a foreign aid bill fell into difficulties, and all foreign aid bills fell into difficulties, it was Johnson, working quietly inside committees of which he was not officially a member, who pulled it back on its feet. When dissident Republicans and Democrats alike attempted to put undue restrictions on the President's purpose to give aid to much unloved areas—say, the Soviet satellites so as to divide the Communist monolith—it was Johnson who most of all defeated those restrictions. When Eisenhower needed congressional support in attempting to approach the Soviet Union to breach the Iron Curtain, it was Lyndon Johnson upon whom, very privately, he called most of all, usually to find that the Senator was already ahead of him.

Generally, Johnson walked in all this with the softest of feet. He had, on the one side, to avoid annoying Senate colleagues officially in charge of foreign affairs by any suggestion of public intervention over their heads. On the other side, he had to do what was necessary for foreign policy, and for Eisenhower the *President* as distinguished from Eisenhower the Republican. And he had to do all this without ever falling captive to the President's purely domestic designs and without giving less informed Democratic colleagues any excuse to cry out that he was trading with the Republican enemy.

Accordingly, a legend grew that he was perhaps a strong "domestic" leader but that he was weak in, or not deeply interested in, world affairs. For the most part he took this as one of the unhappy hazards of his trade, an occupational risk like that of a brilliant ghost writer when his prose wins some other man international renown in the field of letters.

Now and again, however, he rattled the bars of his cage. One night, after an exhausting job in putting through the Senate a foreign policy bill bearing the name of a famous senatorial foreign policy expert who himself was absent from the scene, Johnson went wearily home to find Mrs. Johnson pink with pleasure from an evening spent at an embassy dinner.

She told him that she had had a splendid time and had most appreciated the wit and charm of her escort. "Who was he, Bird?" asked Johnson. It had been the same elderly senatorial foreign policy expert who had not attended the Senate that evening. Johnson for a long moment contemplated this small burlesque of fate in absolute silence. At length he uttered the only possible comment in the circumstances: "Ah, yes; of course."

For years he took the lead in Congress with ways to challenge the Russians to open their society wider and in seeking to forward disarmament, as at least a conceivable means of avoiding atomic holocaust. In June of 1957 he initiated a debate, not greatly noticed by the wide public but deeply involving all factions in the Senate, by this prophetic sentence:

"The intercontinental ballistics missile with a hydrogen warhead is just over the horizon. It is no longer just the disorderly dream of some science fiction writer." He then went on:

We must assume that our country will have no monopoly on this weapon. The Soviets have not matched our achievements in democracy and prosperity; but they have kept pace with us in building the tools of destruction.

With such weapons in a divided world, there will be little choice. We may return to the caves of our remote ancestors and burrow underground like the prairie dogs of west Texas.

There are reasonable alternatives to this unreasonable prospect. They are alternatives which are available to mankind—providing that mankind will adopt them.

Our present situation could have been avoided. Twelve years ago—when we had a monopoly on the atomic bomb—the United States offered to share the secrets of the atom with the entire world.

We asked in return only reasonable guarantees that the atom would never again be used in warfare. This offer had no parallel in history—and it would have converted the atom from an implement of death to an implement of life.

Two years later, this plan was approved by the General Assembly of the United Nations. It was blocked only by the Soviet Union and its satellites.

There is no point in reliving the past. I am not going to waste your time and my time in proving that the Soviets were wrong. Free people, who have had access to the truth, are already aware of the facts.

We live in the present. We no longer have a monopoly on atomic power. But there is a sound reason for recalling the events of 1946 and 1948. One aspect of those events may point the way to the future.

The Russian people have never had an opportunity to weigh the free world's proposal for the control of atomic energy. They were never informed about it openly and frankly. They never knew that Stalin provoked an arms race that, if continued, must end in the total elimination of mankind.

Today humanity is a great deal closer to self-destruction than it was ten years ago.

And yet, because we are close to the threat, we may also be closer to hope. I do not foresee any quick Utopian solutions. A happy ending to the atomic-hydrogen menace will not be easily found.

But I am convinced, to borrow Churchill's phrase, that if we cannot see the beginning of the end, we can at least see the end of the beginning.

There are pathways of peace and progress open to all humanity. The statesmen of the world have one over-riding duty —to help light those paths.

Where lie the signs of hope? They lie in the realm of reason.

The challenge is truly immediate. It involves actions that can and must be taken this year, now—during the remaining 206 days of 1957.

Our basic need goes by the technical name disarmament. That long, rather dull-sounding word represents a host of complicated problems. The answer—even a beginning to the answer—represents the hope of all mankind.

We must initiate action on five objectives, each contributing to our crusade for disarmament.

1. Controlled reduction of military forces by all countries.

2. A start on a mutual "open skies" foolproof inspection system.

3. A frank and open search for a method of suspending tests of the bigger nuclear weapons, under airtight conditions which give full protection against violations.

4. A reduction of everyone's stockpile of nuclear weapons

and means for delivery under copper-riveted methods of mutual inspection.

5. And this is the key to ultimate hope: a world-wide agreement, backed by absolute safeguards, that no nation will make any new fissionable materials for weapon purposes, neither the three present nuclear powers nor those who may soon have the capacity.

How do we launch this program? We do so in the only way possible, in the only way that accords with American traditions.

We must create a new world policy, not just of "open skies," but of open eyes, ears, and minds, for all peoples of the world.

I call for the "open curtain." Let truth flow through it freely. Let ideas cleanse evil just as fresh air cleanses the poisoned, stagnant mass of a long closed cavern.

Mankind's only hope lies with men themselves. Let us insist that the case be submitted to the people of the world.

A few years ago this would have been utterly impractical. But great events have recently stirred the world. We must seize the hopes they suggest. We must not be blinded to those hopes by rigid reflections of the past.

Only four years ago the brutal Stalin died. Only a year ago the world learned that the new Russian leader, Khrushchev, had found it necessary to expose the depths of Stalin's evil. And only six days ago Khrushchev took advantage of America's facilities to come into our homes and state the Communist case.

I am glad that he did so. I have complete trust and faith in our people.

They will not be contaminated by open Communist propaganda.

We should welcome this example of direct argument.

But we must—I think—go farther than this. Let us take

Khrushchev's technique and turn it back upon him. Let us use the program as the means to open the iron curtain.

As he has used our TV screens for his appeals, let us demand to use *his* screens for our appeal—the appeal of truth, undefensive and undismayed.

We should ask Khrushchev to provide us with Soviet-wide uncensored radio and TV facilities. We should call on him to allow spokesmen of our own choosing to come into Russian homes and state our case—the American case—to the Russian people.

Let us get back to fundamentals. Let us return to the principles which made America strong and great and free.

The most important of these principles is that truth can be found in the free marketplace of ideas.

It is no secret that I am a Democrat. My political faith can be traced to many sources. One of them—and the most important of them—was Thomas Jefferson, who said: "I know of no safe depository of the ultimate power of society but the people themselves; and if we think them not enlightened enough to exercise their control with a wholesome discretion, the remedy is not to take it from them, but to inform their discretion by education."

This is an elegant and graceful way of putting a basic truth that I learned in Johnson City, Texas. Stated more simply, it means: never underestimate the intelligence of the people.

Sometimes they are misinformed. Sometimes the truth is withheld from them. But when they have the facts, their judgment will be good and fair and honorable.

I have a deep and abiding faith in the judgment of the people who ride the range in the Texas Hill Country. They may not have the ease of expression and the grace of manner of those who were reared in more settled parts of our land.

But no demagogue is going to lead the lean, spare Texan

who runs the cattle on my ranch into the paths of bigotry. And Nikita Khrushchev is not going to convert him into a Communist.

He's just plain got too much sense. And I don't think that he is unusual. I believe that most Americans are like that.

They may speak with a different accent. They may plow corn land in Iowa or sew clothes in New York City. They may work on the docks in Seattle or run a department store in Kansas City.

They may be Northern Yankees or Southern Rebels. They may be Catholics, Protestant, or Jews. It makes no difference because they are all Americans.

I am not afraid to have them listen to Nikita Khrushchev or Karl Marx or Nicolai Lenin himself. They have the intelligence and the independence to make up their own minds.

I know there are some who are fearful of the effects of Communist propaganda upon our people. I am a Jeffersonian. I do not share those fears.

I favor granting Khrushchev or Bulganin or Molotov or any Soviet leader television time in America every week of the year. I demand in return only that they grant us equal opportunities for reaching the Russian people.

Let the Russians say what they wish. Let our people hear it to the bitter end. I have faith in them. I do not believe that there will be any Communist converts.

I am not talking of a "propaganda offensive" or "waging peace." Those are the terms of advertising, and this country is not interested in making a mercantile item of peace.

I am not talking of merely one reply to Khrushchev by the President or some other official.

I am calling for an open curtain for full discussion of the immediate, urgent problems facing our people. We should insist on the right to state our case on disarmament in detail to the Soviet people. We should have weekly appearances during this year on Soviet radio and television, and we should offer similar facilities here.

We should not let a single day pass without raising the issue. We should call it up in the United Nations; we should make it a basic proposal in all disarmament talks; we should insist upon it every time a Russian representative is within earshot.

Why not allow Soviet labor leaders to talk to our people in return for our labor leaders talking to theirs? Why not allow Soviet industrial managers to talk to our people in return for our industrialists talking to theirs?

Is there any good reason why American and Soviet farmers should not exchange views—in the plain sight of the whole world? Is there any reason why our scholars and our professional men should be barred from mutual exchange with their Soviet counterparts?

Let the people know!

Let truth shine through the open curtain!

And when the people know, they will insist that the arms race, the nuclear explosions, the intercontinental missiles all be banished. They will insist upon systems that safeguard us against world suicide.

Still, Johnson's foreign policy leadership all during Eisenhower's administration—and indeed through all his time as Democratic leader—was largely exercised, by choice and by what he believed to be necessity, inside the Senate. His public speeches on the subject were very rare; his public appearances even rarer. Indeed, the only time he ever went officially to the United Nations in those years was in 1958, when, at President Eisenhower's request, he presented a United States resolution calling for peaceful exploration of outer space.

This mission was hardly avoidable, either on Eisenhower's part or Johnson's, for the senator had guided to passage the pioneer act by which this country went into the space program, a program now vastly increased and productive, of which he would later be policy chairman during the Kennedy administration. Not since his struggle for military preparedness as a young congressman has any issue preoccupied Johnson as much as has the peaceful conquest of space. The problem still absorbs him, as he made plain in one of his first presidential messages to Congress.

11

A STUDY
IN LEADERSHIP

THE DAYS OF SENATE LEADERSHIP were, for Johnson, days of competing tasks and interests, hardly less formidable than are those he now faces as President. Space or no space, open curtains or closed ones, foreign aid or no foreign aid, he could not forget that he was a political leader as well as a legislative leader. He had told the Democratic conference when he was chosen floor leader that while he would tolerate no merely obstructive partisanship against Eisenhower, he did have a thing or two in mind for subsequent elections. He had promised a positive program for the Democrats themselves, and he had predicted that the time was "not too far distant when the Democratic Party will again be in the majority."

He was wrong as to the Presidency; it took eight years. But he was strikingly right about Congress. In 1954, when Vice-President Richard Nixon went out on a violent and bitter campaign to try to add to the currently thin Republican congressional majority, Johnson appointed himself, without defining his mission in public, to be Nixon's principal adversary. He went everywhere, but he concentrated on the West. There, Nixon was striking desperately to try to destroy such indispensable liberal Democratic senators as the late Joseph O'Mahoney of Wyoming and James Murray of Montana.

Nixon was taking the "rock 'em-and-sock 'em" campaign line; Johnson was talking gravely of Democratic responsibility and competence, a concept he underlined whenever he spoke. Nixon was also talking of Communist subversion, and casting what the Democrats thought was a general disparagement on the loyalty of their party.

By commonly accepted political estimates, Johnson saved at least six Democratic senators that year. And notably he saved both O'Mahoney in Wyoming and Murray in Montana. Johnson was convinced that Nixon was overreaching himself and that the whole "Communists-in-Government" issue would be rejected by the American people in the congressional elections that fall. He made no issue of Nixon; he simply talked of Democratic plans and purposes in Congress. He presented his party as not only "responsible," his old slogan, but also as devoted to a politics of construction rather than destruction. He was also making up his mind, at this time, that when the election was over he was going to see to it that the Senate condemned Senator Joseph R. McCarthy.

In the meantime, he believed that Democratic answers to every charge by Nixon on the loyalty question were foolishly defensive and should be spurned. Thus, on a hot day in a tabernacle in Wyoming, Johnson was in anguish as Senator O'Mahoney devoted an hour's campaign discourse to a full, brilliantly sound but unavoidably defensive explanation of why he had been the attorney for a man vaguely accused of some sort of "subversion."

Sitting on the platform Johnson fidgeted and sadly rolled his eyes as O'Mahoney went on and on to defend a perfectly decent position needing no defense. At length, Johnson could bear it no longer. He advised O'Mahoney, *sotto voce,* to drop that case and go into what he intended to do for Wyoming. O'Mahoney, understandably wound up, at first shrugged off the advice but at length submitted. When he finished, Johnson fairly leapt to the wooden platform and, in a low, purely conversational tone of voice told the people of Wyoming what O'Mahoney had done and could do for them and for decent liberalism.

The outcome of the 1954 Congressional elections was a Democratic triumph, in the face of the rarely matched popularity of President Eisenhower, and in the 1955 session it elevated Johnson from Senate minority to Senate majority leader. It was also a vindication of his strategy of "not biting at Eisenhower," whose own popularity in the country was not in the slightest injured by what had happened to his party in Congress. And the Democrats, under the Johnson-Rayburn leadership, were to more than match the feat by returning a Democratic Congress in 1956 despite Eisenhower's re-election by a landslide. Again, they were to win Congress in 1958 and, more narrowly in the 1960 campaign that sent Kennedy to the White House with Johnson as his Vice-President.

Meanwhile, in 1954, there opened for Lyndon Johnson a great and trying year, full of position, power and performance, but also full of fear and tragedy. He returned to Washington from the congressional campaign as the man who more than any other had placed Eisenhower in the position of a President with the personal support of a majority of the people, but a President whose party was in a clear minority in the Congress.

Thereafter, Eisenhower's domestic role was in truth only magisterial. Though his personal popularity remained unchallenged, his control of the United States government was in fact only such as Johnson and the congressional Democrats would allow him. He had lost—permanently, as it turned out—even nominal control of Congress. The bureaucracy, of course, remained in his hands, but the locus of effective power had now shifted from the White House to the Capitol.

Lyndon Johnson as the conquering majority leader of the Senate, with Rayburn as Speaker of the House, undoubtedly could have destroyed the Eisenhower administration in the period between the assembly of the new Democratic Congress in January of 1955 and the end of Eisenhower's second term in 1960. Though he had carried the country by an impressive personal vote in 1952, and would carry it again in 1956, by an even more impressive personal vote, Eisenhower had lost control not merely of Congress but also of the great orthodox heart of the Republican Party.

The Republican leader of the Senate, William F. Knowland of California, became a far more dangerous antagonist to Eisenhower than Johnson ever chose to be. Knowland not only was by deep conviction skeptical of the Eisenhower policy of seeking negotiations with the Soviet Union—a policy which was also Johnson's—but he was clearly troubled by many other things that Eisenhower did or wanted to do.

In all these circumstances Johnson could have ordered and sustained a paralyzing sit-down strike in Congress against the President which would have brought the government to a sterile halt. He had the opportunity; he had the troops; and, from time to time, he had also some provocation. He looked above and beyond all such temptations, however, for many reasons. He believed in and respected the Presidency as an institution. To him it was not a man named Eisenhower who was really involved here. It was a President who was involved, not his party's President, but still the President.

And Lyndon Johnson knew that while the Democrats could gain much transitory satisfaction by humiliating the partisan enemy at home, they would ill serve both their country and their party in the long run by bringing the Eisenhower administration down to ruin. So, he acted responsibly. Eisenhower himself must have sensed this; for his relationship with Johnson was more that of great power meeting great power than of a President and a mere congressional leader. One of President Johnson's still prized possessions is a warm and appreciative letter from Eisenhower. It is unsigned, for dictating it was Eisenhower's last incomplete act immediately before the heart attack, which for a time left this nation in the hands of a regency made up of the White House staff and Vice-President Richard Nixon.

The power balance, in the afterlight of the 1954 Congressional elections, showed Johnson as undoubtedly the second man in the country, who could have been first man had he elected to follow the excited counsels of those Democrats who wanted him to "give Eisenhower hell."

These, as always, pressed Johnson very hard. He responded to their entreaties and demands for "getting tough" with the homely observation that any jackass could kick down a barn but only men could build and keep one.

At all events, the congressional elections of 1954 out of the way, he moved at once to clear up a national stain which had long since been smeared over not only the Democratic Party, its first intended victim, but also over Eisenhower's wing of the Republican Party. General Eisenhower had deplored McCarthyism, but he had never brought himself to the point of attacking it either consistently or head-on. The late Senator Joseph McCarthy, meantime, had enlarged his campaign of terror against alleged Communist subversives of Democratic background to include those whom he called Communist subversives of Republican background. He had, indeed, by now opened a major assault upon the Eisenhower administration itself, and notably upon the United States Army.

Johnson, seeing the moment to be ripe at last for effective counterattack, moved in. He arranged, along with Knowland, the Republican Senate leader, for the creation of a select, strictly bipartisan, Senate committee to investigate McCarthy's actions in the Senate. Never had a high panel of justice been so carefully chosen. Johnson's own Democratic nominees to it were, without exception, men of judicial background or temperament, and, most significantly, of moderate political views. So, too, were Knowland's Republican nominees.

Johnson in the past had discouraged every effort by individual Senators to move for McCarthy's condemnation out of hand and without trial. For this was precisely what McCarthy himself had been doing. He had been condemning men without hearing or trial, with himself, a blazingly biased party in interest, being both judge and jury. What Johnson wanted, and what he got, was an investigating committee free of any record of partisanship against or for McCarthy. Though he wanted a conviction, he also wanted an absolutely fair trial. The two concepts were by no means mutually exclusive, for the trial was to be upon charges subject to the clearest of proof: McCarthy's long and openly contemptuous conduct toward the Senate itself, an institution whose integrity he had repeatedly impugned and whose reputation he had undeniably smirched.

The Select Committee met under the chairmanship of Senator Arthur Watkins of Utah, a Republican and a high Mormon churchman. One of its ablest Democratic members was Senator John Stennis, a Mississippi Democrat with a distinguished judicial past and a man perfectly typifying that impersonal, aseptically fair justice whose maintenance is so infinitely more important even than bringing disorder and violence to book. The Select Committee in due course brought in its bill of indictment—inevitable, given all the facts, but brought in only after fair and exhaustive opportunity for McCarthy to have his full say.

Johnson's purpose, as the leader of the dominant party and as the symbol of the honor of the Senate, was not only fairness but also the full appearance of fairness. It was a proceeding not unlike a general court martial of a high officer by his fellow high officers. They were going to condemn McCarthy, for condemned he had to be on the evidence, but they were going to do it in such a way that all would know that it had been done in order and with decency.

It was a long, acute struggle in the last weeks of the lame duck Republican Congress in the late autumn of 1954. It is not easy now, in a time of a politics of civility for which Eisenhower and Kennedy and Johnson alike must be given credit, to recall or make believable the political scene at that time. We had suffered the enormous shock of the Communist invasion of South Korea, the first open and massive military lunge of international Communism against Western interests since Truman had halted Communist incursions in Greece-Turkey and then, with the Marshall Plan, in western and southern Europe. There had followed the traumatic and tragically divisive national frustration at our policy of limited commitment in Korea which had caused that war of liberation to end at last in a quite unsatisfactory settlement.

Millions in the nation were sullen, fearful and endlessly suspicious that sell-outs in high places, or perhaps even treason, were at work against our policies of Communist containment. Such able and devoted men as General George C. Marshall and Secretary of State Dean Acheson were vilified. A President of the United States himself, Harry S. Truman, despite his military resistance to Communist aggression, was held in angry contempt by many for being "soft on Communism." Into this witches' kettle, Senator McCarthy had introduced a politics of simplistic unreason that had tragically strong appeal in a bewildered, almost neurotic, nation. He seemed to many the one leader against Communism.

It is easy now to underestimate the degree of his support, for he managed to present himself as the sole avenging angel and the sole rightful Cassandra against the evils of the time. There was, as I have said, a long period in which he had terrified his own Republican party and had backed the Democrats into a defensive position. Johnson was one of the few Democrats—there were not many, as it is now sometimes supposed—who amidst this ugly storm, from first to last, had stood in defense of the essential honor of this country, during both the Truman and the Eisenhower administrations.

As Johnson saw them, the essential political problems in the Senate, as at last it came to grips with McCarthy and McCarthyism, were these: to have the act of condemnation end as a national and not a partisan act, and to see to it that the Democratic Party in the Senate showed a massive unity in doing its duty in this crisis for constitutional government, fair play, and public order. He worked as he had never worked before to draw the Democrats together.

The possibility of such unity seemed very remote. McCarthy not only still had strong backing from the right-wing of his party in the Senate; he also had the reluctant toleration of a good many Democrats, notably those from States of heavy Roman Catholic voting strength. One of the unhappiest realities of that time was that McCarthy, a Catholic, was widely believed among politicians to have a special appeal to Catholic voters in traditionally Democratic states. For my own part, as a journalist much active in this issue at the time, I always thought the estimate to be both wrong and insulting to Catholics. It was my be-

lief that the division in this country between pro-Mc-
Carthyism and anti-McCarthyism was not religious, not
economic, not social and not even partisan; that it divided, as no issue had done in my lifetime, those who instinctively understood from those who did not understand
the basic concepts of the British and American systems of
government.

All the same, right or wrong, just or unjust, the notion
existed that to go against McCarthy was to go against the
mores of many Democratic states, if not to take up the position (as Johnson had once grimly described it in another
connection), of resolving that Communism was good for
the United States. Facing all this, Johnson appealed, he
lectured, he "maneuvered," he operated among the Senate
Democrats to persuade them to stand fast.

When at last the Select Committee, under the unyieldingly conservative and also unyieldingly courageous Senator Watkins, brought in its resolution of censure, it met a
determined and undeniably skillful resistance from a
mixed group. There were McCarthy's outright supporters.
There were those who for one reason or another would
tolerate him. And there were those who were simply unwilling to commit the Senate to an act without exact precedent in its history.

Senator Everett M. Dirksen of Illinois—today the Republican leader of the Senate, and a very good one, too—
led the counterattack. He came forward with a substitute
motion to the effect that McCarthy's conduct had not war-
ranted formal censure. Johnson, moving about the Senate
chamber like a commander looking for holes or soft spots
in his line, said little and left the speechmaking to others.

He was not now concerned with talk; he was only concerned that no salient had been left uncovered. The talk went on and on; and then came the vote. Dirksen was thrown heavily back. For his motion to exculpate McCarthy this was the end: it was rejected, sixty-six votes to twenty-one, with nine not voting. Johnson's line had held like stone. Of the forty-three Democrats who voted, forty-three said "no" to the exculpation.

Now came Senator Karl Mundt, Republican of South Dakota, with a motion merely to "disavow and disapprove" certain of McCarthy's acts, but not to condemn or censure him. The result: rejection, seventy-four to fifteen, with seven not voting.

The late Senator Styles Bridges, of New Hampshire, the powerful Republican dean of the Senate, moved forward with yet another proposal to defeat censure. The result: rejection by sixty-eight to twenty, with eight not voting. Again, the Democrats stood together one hundred per cent.

On and on went the struggle, and again and again Johnson held his party firm, until at last came the climax, the final vote on the resolution to condemn. It was adopted sixty-seven to twenty-two, with seven not voting. Again, those Democrats who voted stood one hundred per cent for censure; the Republicans split exactly fifty-fifty. Johnson had won his two objectives. It was demonstrably not a merely partisan action; it demonstrably found the entire voting Democratic Party of the Senate united.

Johnson had made no heroic, empty gesture; he had held his fire until the right moment, and then he had gone in, all guns blazing, and swept the field. No man then in

the Senate, not even among Johnson's usual critics on the
ultra-liberal left, would have contended that day that
any other Senate leader could have managed this *tour de
force*. It was the end for McCarthy. From this moment
on, he was lost and abandoned. Not a single right or privilege of a United States senator had been taken from him;
he was as free as ever to talk and to vote. But when he
voted he only cast one vote; when he talked none listened
any more. An icy aura of Senate displeasure now enclosed
him, and as his power in the Senate crumbled, his following in the country broke and dissolved.

The nation accepted the verdict, and turned to other
affairs. A verdict arrived at in any other way, by a hurried kangaroo court, by any suggestion of unfairness to
McCarthy, would have divided the country it was meant
to save. This was, one believes upon reflection, the sharp-
est single illustration of leadership at once perceptive, sensitive, poised and highly practical, in all the Senate career
of Lyndon Baines Johnson. He passed no bill here; he altered no high policy; he created no innovation. But he
lanced a terrible boil on the body of the United States; he
reclaimed the authority and decency of its public institutions; he vindicated ordered freedom in the nation.

Thus he closed the year 1954, the last year of Republican control of Congress in his time as Senate Democratic
leader, in a flourish of triumph for himself, for his party,
and of belated triumph for the Senate of the United States.
Though he would never have admitted it in public, there
were times, early on, when he might privately have been
as happy had his party remained in the minority. Party
control of the Senate by a single seat inherently forms a

very shaky platform for leadership. So, indeed, does top-heavy control, for then individual senators of the dominant party feel no compulsion to "stay regular," for they can always look about them and say: "If I defect from the leadership here, what matter? Look at all those other available members of the majority."

Johnson's difficulty at the moment, however, was far less subtle; he had too few, not too many, Democrats under his charge. On his right were those faithful personal friends but frequent problem-colleagues, the southerners like Richard Russell of Georgia, Harry Byrd of Virginia, Spessard Holland of Florida, and others. These had not only affection for Johnson, they also had a paternal interest in him and a curiously mixed and modified regional pride in him. If he was often the odd man out as a southerner, he was still a southerner. Sometimes they shook their heads sadly over him, rather in the manner of an old-fashioned southern lady who will never think of reading the young cousin out of the family but will all the same express a certain well-bred regret about him, together with a tolerant amusement at the vagaries of a new generation. In this manner, many southern Senators acted at the unsuitable connections Johnson had formed with such outlandish outfits as, say, the CIO. But while they could not follow him in everything, they would follow him to the last mile permissible under their political circumstances at home.

The great central point is that the Senate (as has been elsewhere observed by this writer at some length) is a highly human place where men are found to be acceptable or unacceptable upon club-like criteria which do not please purist students of political science. The southern elders had no intention of allowing Johnson to fail as majority leader, not even if they had to take some considerable risk back home in supporting him.

On Johnson's left there was a mixed bag of northern, eastern and western Democrats who had originally gone along with his elevation to leadership with some misgivings and who were now far from reassured by his policy of only "responsible" opposition. Some were doctrinaire liberals; some were practical liberals; some were, like Johnson, a pragmatic mixture of liberalism and conservatism. His first objective was to find a means to persuade these varicolored lambs to lie down together.

(He was rightly convinced, meantime, that he could fairly easily persuade the varicolored lions on his right to walk along together without disturbing the air with violent roars against each other.)

Johnson, surely one of the most unautomated politicians of all time, did not undertake this unpromising job upon any theory that he could compromise diverse issues so much as that he could reconcile diverse men and *then* accommodate them to a rough but reasonable consensus upon issues. The human center of his arch of purpose was Senator Hubert H. Humphrey of Minnesota. Humphrey had come to the Senate from the elections of 1948 freighted with so frightening a load of good, extreme-liberal intentions as to make him at once, to the conservatives, typical of the victims of prairie madness whom old Tory Republican Senator George Moses of New Hampshire had once called "Sons of the Wild Jackass."

Still, Humphrey had mellowed, if only a bit, in the intervening years, and now Johnson fixed his restless, reckoning eyes on him. He set out to make of him a practical liberal, correctly believing that if he accomplished this seemingly not likely achievement, he would prove that all Democrats could, in a pinch, "sit down and reason together." The Johnson approach to Humphrey and the Johnson follow-through—call it an "operation" or whatever you prefer—was an amazing thing to watch. First, he convinced Humphrey of his own authentically liberal bonafides—which was not too hard. They were both going the same way; the only difference was that Johnson knew how to get there, or almost there, whereas the Humphrey of that period, like his fellow ultra-liberals, only knew most passionately that he would like to get there.

The next step was to bring Humphrey the human being, as distinguished from Humphrey the ideologue, into camp, not in a crude, deceptive sense but in a real sense. Johnson understood that Humphrey's unacceptability to the Senate patriarchs, and notably to the old southern boys, was neither a pleasant nor a useful fact of life to his younger colleague. For the old boys, however unregarded or poorly regarded in Minnesota, were very well regarded, indeed, in the Senate of the United States. If they could not make or break a young and "out" senator, they could come very close to it. And this Humphrey knew, too.

Soon, Johnson began putting in a casual word now and then, in favor of his protégé-target, with the then Democratic dean of the Senate, Walter F. George of Georgia. "Senator," he would say to George—punctilious of the gulf in both age and tradition that separated the old man from himself—"Hubert isn't such a bad fellow, you know.

On such and such a matter, he has shown a great deal of responsibility and ability." George at first listened to these soft interventions with a bland, mannered reserve which never in him could have been called unpleasant skepticism. At length, however, he himself began to see some pretty good things in young Humphrey. And at last he went the incredible distance, in a mellow mood one day, of publicly declaring that Humphrey really ought to be returned to the Senate by his people.

The upshot was that Humphrey was transformed from a much-talking but little-succeeding senator to one of real power in the actual operation of the Senate. Nobody had lost any principles; nobody had abandoned any convictions. But Johnson had not merely added a recruit to his policies; he had also given a new proof that men could, in truth, "sit down and reason together."

Thus, as one legislative issue after another approached and was mastered—never perfectly and sometimes only meagerly—he kept his thin Democratic majority in a degree of unity no Democratic majority in the Senate, large or small, had known in many years. A Byrd of Virginia— a genteelly implacable foe of a good deal of all that had happened since and even during the Roosevelt administration—could and would operate amicably sometimes with the oddest vis-à-vis. It might even be Senator Wayne Morse of Oregon, a maverick from the Far West who made the quasi-populists of Johnson's southwest Texas youth look rather like members of the Union League Club in Philadelphia.

And at the same time, Johnson formed an agreeable working relationship with Knowland, the Republican leader, so that between them they could keep the Senate on the track, in the housekeeping sense, avoiding that sterile quarrelsomeness into which sometimes that body can fall, if the leaders do not hold the reins reasonably tightly on both sides of the aisle.

Knowland and Johnson, of course, agreed very rarely on issues. They agreed almost all the time, however, on the proprieties and on their common wish to see the Senate function. They also were at one in their hostility to a politics of mere violence and recrimination. For example, in 1954, while Richard Nixon was on the stump calling Democrats some very ugly names on the subversive issue, Knowland once rose stolidly from his seat to disavow and strongly disapprove of some of the things the Vice-President had been saying.

The Johnson-Knowland bargain was implicit but very real: disagree they would and did; pick at each other over non-essentials they would not and did not. They were a fascinatingly different pair as they sat, separated by two feet of Senate aisle, on their front chairs in the chamber. Knowland, big, heavy, infinitely correct, was grave, measured in word and movement, stiffly in his place and rarely looking back at his troops to the rear. Johnson, tall, casual, and often lounging back on his spine, was forever moving about among his people; now jocular, now chiding, always among them and always alert to their moods, whether moods of weakness or of strength. He dealt with the Senate staff people, down to the pages, with an air of brusque camaraderie, and he gave them a great deal of leeway in their actions so long as they did their jobs. Knowland walked among such people ponderously; not unkindly, but clearly and quite unconsciously drawing a line between their positions and his.

To Johnson's constant railleries, Knowland would respond with slow, pleased grins; though a man of integrity, he was not a man of ease. To watch the two was sometimes like watching a mastiff and a hunting dog. Knowland, to change the metaphor, played it by the book; Johnson played it "from the back of his neck." It was, nevertheless, a memorably decent association between this able, courageous, inflexible and carefully orthodox Republican and this able, courageous, endlessly inventive and, sometimes, quite unclassifiable Democrat.

Occasional rebellions against Johnson were being talked of here and there all through the year 1955—sometimes by ultra-liberal senators who held their seats in part because he had campaigned so strenuously for them —but they never came to anything. The unarguable success of his leadership was a compelling practical argument for its soundness, or, at a minimum, for its necessity. When revolts were whispered about, Johnson met them in silence. He never sought overtly to punish a man for being, by his standards, a bad Democrat, but he never overlooked an opportunity to reward a man whom he considered a good Democrat.

The Senate under Johnson's restless prodding was turning out work as it had never done before, and as summer succeeded spring, the majority leader's working day was rarely less than eighteen hours. He was amassing an incredible record of legislative performance, but he was driving himself too hard.

On July 2, a Saturday, he decided to take a rare, brief, weekend off at the country place near Middleburg, Virginia, of old friends, George and Herman Brown. Sitting in the official limousine on the way down to Middleburg, he felt ill and there were sudden, sharp pains in his right arm and shoulder. He believed he had indigestion; what he had in fact was a massive heart attack. He was hurriedly brought back to Washington and thence to the naval hospital at Bethesda, Maryland. His wife was waiting when the ambulance arrived at the hospital. His friends feared that it was the end for him; he, too, was wryly prepared for that eventuality.

He arranged for Senator Earle Clements of Kentucky, then the Democratic Senate whip, to take over the leadership, his first thought being that the Senate must go on. He directed that the press be notified candidly of his condition and outlook. He tried to joke with Mrs. Johnson as he was taken into the hospital. Then there opened a desperate battle for his life, into which he himself threw all his determination. Within a few days he had commandeered part of a wing in the hospital where some of his staff set to work. For he was preparing either to close out his affairs in good order, if death was to be his fate, or to be ready to resume them in good order, if he continued to live.

He won the great struggle; there was no recurrence of heart spasm, and years later the most careful and repeated examinations by physicians would show him unmarked.

In December, the doctors gave him word that he could return to the Senate. He had stopped smoking cigarettes, of which once he had used three packs a day, and he began to watch his diet somewhat under the persistent monitorship of Mrs. Johnson. Otherwise he was, and would remain, really unchanged.

12

CIVIL RIGHTS

THE PRESIDENTAL YEAR 1956 WAS now at hand and Johnson, again astride the Senate with all his old mastery, was being talked of for President. He did not take this talk very seriously, but he was deeply concerned that the Democratic unity so painfully forged in the Senate should not be destroyed by the inevitable divisiveness of the coming presidential contest.

The renomination of Adlai E. Stevenson by the Democrats, notwithstanding his heavy defeat by General Eisenhower four years before, was a strong probability. Harry Truman, however, was known not to be keen for Stevenson. There was, in short, a strong prospect for an ugly and divisive intra-party fight at the coming national convention.

Johnson and Rayburn, meantime, had long since become the party's two highest national leaders holding elective office. They were the principal makers of the Democratic record since 1952, and so they felt a deep responsibility for holding the party together, through the convention and the campaign. Few realistic observers believed that Stevenson, or any other conceivable Democratic nominee, for that matter, could win. The real need was to prevent the party from falling into a shambles after the anticipated defeat in November.

In all these circumstances Johnson became himself a candidate, or really a quasi-candidate, at the convention. It was not his purpose to obtain the nomination for President, which was quite out of the question, but to husband the party; and to see to it that the platform did not offer intolerable outrage, as distinguished from mere unwelcome declarations, to any major party element. In these objectives he succeeded.

Though Stevenson went down to the predicted defeat before Eisenhower, the Democrats returned to Congress in stronger force than before. Johnson then began to prepare the magnum opus of his legislative career, the Civil Rights Act of 1957. For a century the civil rights issue had dogged, bedeviled and divided, along the Mason-Dixon Line, a Democratic Party in Congress which in recent years under his leadership had stood more and more together on other issues. How divisive the thing had been no man knew so well as Johnson. Moreover, he had never been comfortable, as a man springing from a western pocket in the South, with racial discrimination. He thought it wrong. He thought it humanly wasteful. He thought it increasingly intolerable in political terms, as well. And he thought that in spite of all his own southern political connections, and in a sense *because* of them, he had a duty to act as a national leader and the requisite skill to do so.

As early as March of 1949, as the then very new and junior senator from Texas with a plurality of less than a hundred votes in his pocket, he had gone on record:

Perhaps no prejudice is so contagious or so unreasoning as the unreasoning prejudice against men because of their birth, the color of their skin, or their ancestral background. Racial prejudice is dangerous because it is a disease of the majority endangering minority groups. . . . For those who would keep any group in our nation in bondage I have no sympathy or tolerance. Some may feel moved to deny this group or that the homes, the education, the employment which every American has a right to expect, but I am not one of those.

My faith in my fellow man is too great to permit me to waste away my lifetime burning with hatred against any group. I believe that we have a system of representative government which is strong enough, flexible enough and fair enough to permit all groups to work together toward a better life.

Then in 1954 every Senator from the old Confederate South save Johnson had signed a "Southern Manifesto" protesting the Supreme Court's decision that separate but equal school facilities for the races were unconstitutional. Many of his best personal friends were signatories. In refusing to go along with them, Johnson parted wholly and forever from the deepest mores of southern Senate politics. The late liberal Democratic Senator Richard Neuberger of Oregon called this "one of the most courageous acts of political valor I have seen take place in my adult life."

But though it was, indeed, an act of courage, it was other things as well. Johnson, who is invariably more sensitive to criticism from his left than from his right, but who is also invariably sadder when he has to break with *personal* friends from his right than from his left, believed his responsibilities as leader of *all* the Senate Democrats would have prohibited him from adopting the sectional view of the Manifesto, even if he had not considered it wrong in principle. To sign would not have imperiled his leadership in the technical sense, since he was by now quite strong enough to throw off any possible effort actually to unseat him. It would, however, have opened that leadership to endless challenge and, indeed, would have compromised it. There was also the fact of self-interest; enlightened self-interest, to be sure, but self-interest all the same.

A man holding national office in the Democratic Party, and to him the Senate leadership was precisely this, could not join an assault upon the Supreme Court of the United States and expect to maintain that leadership morally intact. Too, there was in him the unsleeping memory of that other minority group in Texas which had "gone to the bridge with him"—the Mexican-Americans—and there was the lifelong and genuine racial and religious tolerance which was a part of him and of his father before him.

Finally, certain vague and somewhat ambivalent presidential aspirations were by now stirring in him. These aspirations, it seemed on very close and continuous observation of him in that period, were both thin and wavering. But they did exist. The essential skepticism and sense of realism which are very strong strains in the bottom areas of his private character told him that he could never make "the big job" more often than his in-and-out sense of optimism told him that perhaps he could.

But more than anything else, perhaps, he was motivated by accumulating disgust at what he considered quite rightly to be generations of congressional demagoguery on the whole civil rights question. In Congress after Congress, professional civil rightists had come in crying for bills so extreme in their scope and so blind to the infinite human complications of this tragic issue left by the Reconstruction as to carry within themselves only the seeds of futility and failure.

In Congress after Congress, professional anti-civil rightists had stood upon equally demagogic barricades in proud "resistance" to something that was not going to happen anyhow. The cant in this matter over the long years had built up in Congress a kind of ugly atoll of cynicism, like a reef of rubbish, which persistently stood in the way of any sensible solution of a great and bitter national problem. It also persistently stood in the way of greatly needed legislation in a dozen fields. Wherever one turned, to housing, to rural electrification, to public relief, even to military preparation, with its necessary draft of men for service, always Topic A would intrude. The violent, catch-poll professional civil rightists would insist upon anti-discrimination riders to almost any progressive measure of public importance. This only led to defeat or dilution of the bill, for there was always the certainty that its right-wing opponents would seize this opportunity to make cynical "civil rights" coalitions with their left-wing opposite numbers, whom otherwise they detested, and so destroy the capacity of the moderate and reasonable center to act at all.

At any rate, Johnson now determined to make a truly effective challenge to the old Congressional tradition that nothing could be done about civil rights. Many had talked very loudly about doing something but nobody,

not even Franklin Roosevelt or Harry Truman, if it came
to that, had ever really tried to do much in the only sense
that counted, the legislative sense.

All this was the backdrop of the scene as, in July of 1957,
the House of Representatives passed and sent to the Senate an Eisenhower administration civil rights bill. Civil
rights bills had repeatedly before this been passed in the
House, whose iron rules and limitation upon debate can
bring through the most bitterly contested measure, given
a convinced majority of one. The Senate, now as always,
was the main problem. The heart of this bill was to em-
power the federal government to intervene on behalf of
any person, with or without his consent, whose civil rights
had either been denied or threatened. These large sanctions would have been implemented by authorizing the
Department of Justice to bring actions for federal injunctions against actual or threatened violations. Those dis-
obeying injunctions could be held in criminal contempt
by a federal judge sitting without a jury, and punished to
the extent of the judge's own determination.

Now, however good the intention, this was a federal
writ that would run very far, indeed. What was being
contemplated was the definition of a novel federal crime,
to be tried without jury protection and punished by a
judge without established limitations upon him. Moreover, it was a grant of power to the Attorney-General without precedent, and again, without limitation. A corrupt
or overly ambitious Attorney-General, indeed, could find
civil rights violations where none existed to other eyes.
And he could, in theory anyway, bring a series of actions
against local officials anywhere, endlessly tying them up

in court and in fact all but paralyzing all local exercise of power. And all of this could be done without at any point bringing in the ancient protection to accused persons of the right of jury trial.

The Supreme Court in its integration decree had called only for "all deliberate speed" and had specifically and designedly left a large authority to the judgment of local school authorities and local federal courts to implement the decision in their own way. The House measure, it was feared by many of the most authentically pro-civil rights senators, might permit an over-eager Attorney-General to move prematurely with heavy boots, attempting to force a reform which must, after all, ultimately rest on the good-will and fairness of the local authorities.

If all this was too gloomy and overstated a view of the meaning of the House bill, it was at any rate the undoubted consensus then of a majority of the Senate, formed as it had watched the House in its brief deliberations. The Southerners in the Senate, of course, went much farther in their jeremiads. On July 2, 1957 the untitled Southern leader, Senator Russell of Georgia, Johnson's old friend and sometimes friendly enemy, rose with "infinite sadness" to denounce the House bill as "a force measure" upon the South, reminiscent of the days of Reconstruction.

"God give us strength!" he cried out from the Senate floor, "Each and everyone of us [the southerners] will now demean himself as a man, as our people expect us to do, as this cause proceeds."

Johnson, in his seat on the front row, stayed silent, letting the anger and the emotion spend itself, and letting the Republicans, for now, carry the burden of "Eisenhower's bill." He had prepared the most complicated, and the most indispensable, legislative strategy of his career. The Republican Senate leader, Knowland of California, was the leader for the administration. He carried with him the undoubted support of a liberal splinter of the Republican Party in the Senate, plus the larger splinter formed by the Democratic left. Johnson, implicitly in command of the Democrats at the center and slightly right of center, but of no others, reserved his position. He foresaw that the Knowland coalition would not last long, for Knowland's orthodox Republican party troops had no stomach for the combat and the Democratic far left would not long accept Knowland's leadership.

It required fifteen days to bring the Senate to the point of agreeing formally to take up the House measure, which in these fifteen days it had been informally "discussing." Here came the first showdown, to divide those who really meant to act in the end from those who did not. On July 17 a motion to take up was carried, with Johnson and three other "new" southerners—his colleague from Texas, Senator Ralph Yarborough, the late Senator Estes Kefauver of Tennessee, and Senator Albert Gore, also of Tennessee—voting "aye."

The new South was now beginning to move against the total opposition of the old. By July 19 fissures had begun to appear within the Knowland coalition. The Democratic far left withdrew in pain and anger when President Eisenhower, at a press conference, intimated that perhaps the House bill *had* gone too far and that perhaps some compromise was now acceptable.

This was the moment for which Johnson had been waiting. He moved at once into obvious, if still unofficial,
leadership for an amended bill which would put aside for
the time being the unattainable in behalf of the attainable
and desperately needed. The unattainable was the granting at this stage of unlimited federal injunctive power
over school integration. There was simply not a Senate
majority to agree to this; indeed, to press the point to the
end would be to destroy all hope of *any* civil rights progress at that session of Congress, at least.

The attainable was the very strong protection to voting
rights guaranteed in the House bill. For this, Johnson was
resolved to fight to the end; for this, he believed, was not
only the most presently attainable, but also by far the
most important, right that could be assured to the American Negro. Given the vote, all else would come in time,
for the Negro himself would then powerfully help to see to
it.

And now the Johnson troop was expanded from his old
following at the center and slightly to the right of center.
Now some of the erstwhile Democratic left came over to
him, no longer willing to follow Knowland, but also no
longer willing to follow the Democratic far left, whose demands were now moving out of the area of the possible
and rational. Liberal and moderate Republicans, too, began, if rather furtively, to range themselves behind him.

What he was most of all trying to do was to avoid an
all-out Southern filibuster which could have destroyed all
possibility of any effective action. This he did by opening
a process of division among his southern colleagues between those (actually in a majority) who had always

been uncomfortable at denial of so basic a right as that to vote, and those who were determined, from unshakeable habit and prejudice, to stand to the end against anything at all for the Negro. Johnson had completely lost the Democratic far right here. Nor could he depend in any pinch on the Democratic far left, which was now only shouting slogans and catchwords, unconsciously falling right into the trap of the far right, whose aim was no legislation at all.

Thus as the power ratios in the Senate profoundly shifted, two of Johnson's authentic but practical liberal associates, Senators Clinton Anderson of New Mexico, a Democrat, and George Aiken of Vermont, a Republican, moved to the necessary surgical operation. They moved to strike from the bill, in order to save its life and in order to retain and protect its vital voting rights section, the section allowing federal injunctions in school integration questions. This was the first truly critical battle, and when it was over Johnson's policy had won, by fifty-two to thirty-eight.

On July 26 momentum was established for an effective voting rights bill; but now trouble arose over the House provision denying a jury trial even in criminal contempt cases arising from its enforcement. It was not the southerners who became the critical mass here; it was young and old Democratic liberals, principally from the Far West, who could not accept this departure from traditional American jurisprudence. Such lifelong advocates of civil rights for minorities as the late Senator Joseph C. O'Mahoney of Wyoming, one of the great old liberals of the Senate, could not and would not go this far. Some of the great labor unions, moreover, remembering the anti-strike injunctions of the old days when a federal judge was also jury, feared this provision.

So at length the Senate made a compromise: wherever civil contempt was involved, a judge alone could fix the penalty, since the purpose of civil contempt action is not primarily to punish but only to force compliance with court orders. When, however, the case involved criminal contempt—that is, where the purpose of the citation was punitive and not simply corrective—a jury trial would be guaranteed. The objections to this were clear. It was argued with great force that southern juries would not convict for a criminal contempt arising from local refusal to submit to a federal injunction. The traditionalists, however—and again these were more typified by western senators who really wanted an advance in civil rights than by southerners opposing all such action—retorted that maintenance of an unqualified right to jury trial in *any* criminal case was so important as to become the indispensable factor in the issue. Their view became the undoubted view of the Senate. On August 2 the right of jury trial was sustained by a vote of fifty-one to forty-two. Among those standing with the majority was Senator John F. Kennedy. Although he was under heavy pressure from civil rights groups to go the whole way, in the end he could not in conscience do so.

Thus, on August 7 the Senate approved its own version of civil rights, a version which at length was accepted by the House, and became law. On August 30 the bill was sent to President Eisenhower for his signature.

Nothing had been added to the federal government's

power to enforce school integration, but powerful sanctions against denial of the right to vote had been embedded into American law, and the way had been opened for subsequent legislation to extend these sanctions into every area of civil rights. It was a half-loaf, to be sure; but it was an historic half-loaf, indeed, since no bread at all had been available from Congress in more than eighty years.

And no real southern filibuster had, from first to last, been attempted for two reasons: Johnson had divided the southerners by the excision of injunctive sanctions for school integration and so had drawn the "modern" southerners to his side. He had by the same process destroyed what would have been a covert but effective filibuster among the orthodox Republicans. These latter were in truth themselves deeply opposed, though never so candidly as the irredentist orthodox southern Democrats, to putting the injunction into the school integration field, at least until much more time had been allowed for what it was hoped would be orderly southern submission to the Supreme Court's doctrine of "all deliberate speed." Nor had Johnson ever committed himself in the debate against further sanctions in the school area, should these later become demonstrably necessary.

The fight was, among other things, an extraordinary illustration of that highly sophisticated form of politics-by-consent which had long been Johnson's highest expertise. For the job had been accomplished in the most sophisticated political forum in this country, and perhaps in the world, the United States Senate. At the 1956 Democratic convention the year before, Johnson had not appeared at his best as a politician, for the good reason that his capacity to persuade highly informed fellow politicians has always been far higher than his capacity to score well in argument before a wide public. He is, to put it another way, invariably at the top of his form in dealing with those who know him best and with those, in general, to whom politics at the end is more a rational than an emotional enterprise. National conventions are no places for careful examination of the fine print; a legislative assembly exists for that purpose.

Thus Johnson's performance in the Senate was an enormous success with the well-informed, but not necessarily with the general public. Its core of importance, of course, lay not so much in what had actually been done, though what had been done was a great deal. It lay in the fact that the Senate had at last been persuaded to move significantly upon the issue, after nearly a century of double-edged demagogic inaction.

And Johnson had kept his own position open enough to permit him, when he succeeded to the Presidency, to demand enactment of the far wider civil rights bill, initiated by Kennedy and fully concurred in by his successor, when he opened the 1964 legislative year.

The years since 1957 had given at least a pragmatic justification for a far harder bill than either the Senate collectively or Johnson personally had been willing to accept in 1957. Racial disorder had moved from the South to the North, and men who heretofore had been unwilling to grant unprecedented federal sanctions against discrimination in private business, for example, now began to consider these and other far-reaching steps as well.

The 1957 decision to knock out the injunctive weapon in school integration, however, caused many to complain of Johnson's "compromises." He had by no means surrendered any principle. Such distinguished advocates of civil rights as Dean Acheson and Benjamin Cohen publicly stated at the time that the section of the bill in question was loosely drawn and full of unfathomable implications. They saw its abandonment, in the circumstances, as "an unmitigated gain" to the larger cause of protecting voting rights.

Still, the fact remained that the ultra-liberals felt that Johnson had, in this instance, put them on a pretty thin diet. And, their merely glandular hostility to him quite aside, they had a point in one sense. For while their howling on the issue had been essentially irrational, since they sought an end both unsound and unattainable, the fact remained that here, as elsewhere, they had served a useful purpose, to a degree, simply because they *had* been yowling so long even though, in some cases their cries were more intended to catch urban minority group votes than to attain a solution. Their role had been in this sense the classic one of the hammer on the anvil, Johnson in this case, as in a good many others, having been the anvil. If they had never really understood him—and Heaven knows they never had—it was also true that his whole nature, his whole highly rational, highly pragmatic, sense of political operation, prevented his really understanding *them.*

His deep attachment to the art of the possible made him impatient, and sometimes unduly so, with extreme liberals. He recoiled from their shrillness; they recoiled from what they believed to be his rather dark form of candor. He disliked making vast promises; they distrusted the sense of political caution and personal reserve in him that caused this dislike. They thought him crude; he thought them precious and full of cant. So he did not receive from them a fraction of the credit he deserved for wisely accomplishing truly liberal designs; and they did not receive from him the degree of credit to which they were entitled for insistence on their ideal.

13

VICE-PRESIDENT

So LONG AS HE REMAINED MAJORITY
leader this was, in regard to Johnson and the left, the state
of affairs. His inauguration as Vice-President, however,
made him in the extreme liberals' view a "new man" after
a time, whereas to himself he was simply the same man
now removed to another constituency. As the leader of
the Senate he had above all to keep a workable Democratic
Party consensus, a quite simple point which they never
quite seemed to grasp. As vice-president of the United
States his responsibility was no longer to deal subtly with
that difficult institution, the Senate. Now it was solely to
forward the policies of the Kennedy administration, including a few which, given free choice in a theoretical
world, Johnson would never have initiated. He had set
out, remember, to be first of all a *loyal* Vice-President.

Johnson himself, for example, would never as president
have openly attacked Big Steel as Kennedy did in breaking its effort to raise prices. He would have accomplished
his objective not by Kennedy's one naked display of
power, not by assaulting the companies' *right* to make
such management decisions, but rather by working within
the steel community itself to persuade enough companies

that their competitive interests would best be served by refusing to follow Big Steel's price rise.

But Kennedy's civil rights program was definitely one to which Johnson gave not only his loyalty but also his deepest private approval. One of Kennedy's first acts was to ask his Vice-President to undertake the chairmanship of the President's Committee on Equal Employment Opportunity—or, in simpler language, to wield the federal government's theretofore not very large stick against racial discrimination in hiring practices. Johnson privately flinched, as he told friends. It was not that he opposed the committee's purposes, for these he strongly supported. His fear was that because he was widely considered to be essentially a southerner, any failure of the commission to put more Negroes into industrial jobs would bring the cynical reaction that he had, of course, sabotaged the works. It was not so much that he feared personal criticism as that he feared that the kind of personal criticism likely to come in his case would sour the program and cause Negroes to lose faith in it.

Still, Kennedy insisted and Johnson at length accepted the chairmanship. Now that he had taken it, he was determined to show that it would really work and that he, as its chairman, meant precisely what he said when he spoke of the right to an equal chance in employment. There was also the spur of competition in this endlessly competitive man: His predecessor as Vice-President, Richard Nixon, having held the same post, Johnson was determined to better Nixon's job-placement record, both because he thought it was right to do so, and also because he wanted to give Nixon one in the eye.

These two, Nixon and Johnson, had by now twice been locked in bitter combat—in the 1954 congressional elections and in the 1960 presidential elections—and twice Johnson had come out ahead. He had no slightest intention to finish second in this third and less clear-cut confrontation. Some had likened Nixon to Johnson, when the former was presiding over the Senate as Vice-President and Johnson was running the Senate as majority leader, in the single sense that both were tough and able. Johnson, understandably, did not welcome the analogy, since his brand of toughness had never in his career been exercised at the expense of the reputations of others or, indeed, at the expense of any person with less power than himself or less well-armed for counterattack. Johnson could be, and still is, remorseless in the assault when he believes his target to be big enough; but he has not ever fought below his own weight.

The relationship of the two, never really cordial, although usually formally correct on both sides, was further complicated by the visible if never spoken fact that Eisenhower had paid far more court to the Democratic leader of the Senate than to his own Republican Vice-President. Nor was it improved by the circumstance that Eisenhower seemed actually to like Johnson the better of the two.

Johnson, then, approached the equal employment program with a special determination to succeed, but in awareness that, as he once put it to a friend, he "could never succeed in public." A perfectly realistic politician, he does not, of course, hate headlines; he loves them. But in this matter he saw that he must work below the head-

lines. For the essential problem here was one of conciliation in quietude between management and labor; between
management and labor unions still widely using that "Jim
Crowism" which they had so long and so righteously denounced in the South. To talk much about the business
was to harden attitudes on all sides. It had to be an operation not exactly of stealth, but conducted in low tones.

The committee held no press conferences and issued
no handouts as to its progress because it dared not upset
the delicate balance of conciliation. Within a year, however, it had accomplished much. The number of Negroes
in top government jobs, paying from $9,500 to $20,000 a
year, increased by thirty-five per cent. Middle-level Negro
employment in government rose by twenty per cent. The
committee's machinery investigated 2,312 complaints of
job discrimination from men on government-contract industrial work and resolved sixty-eight per cent in favor of
the complainants. Among seventy-five of the Nation's
largest corporate employers involved in the program,
twenty-five per cent of all new jobs went to Negroes. Pre-
viously all-white jobs were opened to Negroes in petro-
chemical plants in Texas and Louisiana; in steel plants in
West Virginia, Alabama and Texas; in shipyards in California and Mississippi; in food processing plants in Georgia. Plans for "Fair Practices" were signed with 118 international and 338 affiliated local unions to abolish segregated locals, segregated lines of seniority and segregated
apprenticeship programs.

Johnson himself was a study, as the old-fashioned
phrase goes, as all this went on so far from public notice.
Many minority group leaders had long known that his in-

terest in fair employment was both genuine and productive wherever he personally was able to apply it, but the
rank and file among minorities had never known it.
Greatly would he have liked to open up his operations to
all-out public relations treatment; for he was anxious to
have the rank and file know what he was really doing, so
that its opinion of him would be altered. But he couldn't
do this without hurting the program. So perforce he
adopted the policy once urged by Winston Churchill in
regard to the doctrine of unconditional surrender in the
Second World War: "Think of it always; speak of it never."
Johnson did, in fact, badly beat Nixon's record in this
field; but few knew it, and the few who did, did not go out
of their way to spread the news.

As Vice-President, Johnson wore five official hats in public—and a sixth and unofficial one in private as a political
and legislative adviser to President Kennedy, second in
influence only, but most definitely, to Attorney-General
Robert F. Kennedy, the President's brother. Johnson was,
of course, constitutionally the president of the Senate. He
was a member of the National Security Council, the country's highest body for the conduct of foreign and military
affairs. He was chairman of the National Aeronautics and
Space Council, and, as already discussed, chairman of the
President's Committee on Equal Employment Opportunity.

He attended meetings of the Security Council and of
the Cabinet and the weekly conferences which the President held with the Democratic congressional leaders. At
the end, however, his principal services to Kennedy were
in domestic politics and legislation and, notably, in for-

eign affairs. As Kennedy's special agent, he traveled to thirty foreign countries, making 150 speeches, and ran up a foreign air mileage of 111,000.

These were not good-will missions or the cornerstone-laying sort of thing. They were vital trips in which Johnson went for broader purposes than to estimate and to report on nearly all the foreign crises which arose in the almost three years of his Vice-Presidency. Kennedy gave his Vice-President wide powers to negotiate and to act on behalf of the United States. A letter from him to Johnson in 1962 indicated the closeness of the relationship.

THE WHITE HOUSE
WASHINGTON

September 26, 1962

Dear Lyndon:

I've not only read but fully digested your report. As I mentioned earlier, I followed your trip closely and regard it as a great success, not least from the standpoint of clarifying our purposes and emphasizing our new policies.

These exercises in personal diplomacy give us a means of putting our administration's stamp on foreign policy which is simply not open to us via normal diplomatic means. The results speak for themselves.

I wish I could share more of the burden of such trips with you, as I know they must often seem a chore. But you're a prisoner of your own success, and I hope I can count on you to take on more such travels when occasion demands.

As for the matters you raise in your report, I am grateful for your insights and find myself generally in accord. I'm sending your report to Dean Rusk, and have asked MacBundy and Bob Komer to insure all suitable follow-through.

Sincerely,

JOHN F. KENNEDY

McGeorge Bundy was, of course, Kennedy's foreign policy adviser in the White House, a position he retained under Johnson, and Bob Komer was Bundy's deputy. The mission involved was Johnson's urgent meeting with a dozen national and religious leaders in the Middle East on the subject of American aid to that region. A great deal more than this subject, however, came up before the conversations had concluded.

Johnson's "personal diplomacy," to which Kennedy referred here, was undertaken with more difficulties than his presidential chief knew. Lower-rank State Department advisers accompanying him persistently sought on his early trips to have Johnson conform to a rather Congress-of-Vienna notion as to the proper behavior of a Vice-President in a foreign land. Johnson, who knew his purposes and Kennedy's purposes a good deal better than his advisers, as persistently insisted upon "meeting the folks." Nearly everywhere he went he drew vast crowds; and he went among them, shaking hands and asking interested questions.

The young State Department types, observing this with horror, thought it almost as bad as "domestic politics." Johnson saw it for what it was. On more than one occasion abroad he mixed and mingled not merely because he liked to, but because he wanted to demonstrate to a hesitant or skeptical head of state with whom he was dealing the essential public popularity of the United States. He was never foolish enough to suppose that the approving throngs hugged him for being a man named Lyndon Johnson; he knew they hugged him because he was Vice-President of a nation which they respected. He carried the symbols of his office very lightly, but he never forgot them, or whom he represented, although he carried them in *his* way. Impatiently shaking off the timidly restraining hands of his American escorts, he once carried foreign aid down to the individual level when he personally arranged for the shipment of an inexpensive American gasoline pump to a peasant in Pakistan whom he found drawing water from a well as they had once done it in Johnson City—with a rope, a pulley, and a bucket.

Before his accession to the Vice-Presidency, Johnson had never traveled widely abroad. Now he saw at first hand the fruits, and sometimes the thorny growths, of American foreign policies which he had helped in Congress to form through the years. He also grasped, as he had never had the opportunity to grasp before, the great central truth that in world politics, just as in politics at home, it is men who make issues and not, except in very rare cases, issues that make men.

He has an incredible capacity to divine other men's real purposes, hidden strengths and weaknesses, their going points and sticking points, even in seemingly casual meetings. But they must be head-to-head meetings, with supernumeraries either absent or pushed into the wings. This gift now became an American diplomatic weapon of no mean power. Kennedy used it widely and never underrated it even though there were frequent complaints from some American diplomats at the Vice-President's terrifying scorn of protocol and calm disregard for the ordinary drill of diplomatic negotiation.

And Johnson's steel-cold private estimates to Kennedy of what this or that foreign leader was really like, and was really likely to do in this or that eventuality, were far more important in deciding the President's actions than was ever publicly known.

The Vice-President got along better with heads of state or government than with ministers and ambassadors. This was particularly true with officers who were more or less freely chosen politicians, familiar with the vast difference between elective power and the secondary power held by appointed men. For he carried with him membership in an international club of practical, which is to say of elective, politicians. These talk of the realities of government, at bottom the realities of power: who has it, and how much, and to what probable end it will be applied.

Years ago, when he was in the Senate, Johnson would sometimes drop in upon the Foreign Relations Committee as an ostensibly meek visitor to its deliberations on those occasions when a genuinely sticky world problem was on the agenda. He would look about him with an air of hesitant apology, as if to say "Now don't let an outsider like me intrude upon you experts too far; I am only here to learn." He would take his seat at the end of the committee table and as the witness, say a Secretary of State, went on with his presentation, Johnson would listen for a while with that still, tense attentiveness that typifies him when a tricky and dangerous matter is afoot.

As a non-member of the committee he would sit dutifully quiet, until the point was reached where he felt the committee was identifying a great many individual trees with almost excessive expertise but was quite missing a definition of the forest which they formed. Then, casting aside his spurious meekness, he would loudly clear his throat and say, "Now, Mr. Chairman, if I may just butt in here a moment!" He would fix the witness with a cold eye and demand: "Now, Mr. Secretary, to cut this down to some size [meaning to cut the cackle] what you are really saying is this, is it not?" The witness, who had not meant to be nearly so blunt and would certainly not have been required to be in Johnson's absence, would look both pained and reluctantly approving of his interrogator's instinct for reaching the kernel of the business. Then he would say, "Well, yes, Senator. . . ."

It was this approach that Johnson took in his foreign travels; and it was this approach that he evoked from his vis à vis. At his first meeting with Charles de Gaulle in Paris on a mission for Kennedy, the old General fixed Johnson with the world's most imperious eye and said to him, unutterably to crush this mere local politician from some absurd place like Texas: "Now, Mr. Johnson, what have you come here to *learn from us?*" Johnson, feeling at home with this method of upmanship which he himself had a hundred times practiced, beamed and replied: "Why, General, simply everything you can possibly teach me." A part of him did not, of course, relish the General's haughtiness; but a greater part of him respected it. And all of him understood it; he was on hard personal ground with the General, but it was at any rate ground on which he knew how to walk. Johnson put the incident away in his mind not as a snub and an irritant but as a small dividend in knowledge: He had learned in the most personal and experienced way, the way he likes to learn things of importance, that this Frenchman was vain, that he was arrogant, that he was strong, that he was able and honorable, and that he was, withal, entirely candid and not given to any oblique approach in going after what he wanted.

No man actually likes to be "told off" by others; but Johnson tolerates the process far better than most, and turns it to his own ultimate advantage in a surprising number of cases, if he respects the teller-off. Moreover, this sort of toughness can become, for him, the basis of a prickly, sardonic friendship. In the old days in the Senate the most authentically tough Republican leader he ever confronted in his career was the late Senator Styles Bridges of New Hampshire. When Johnson was first elected to the Democratic leadership, Bridges called on him in his chambers, sat down across the table, looked straight at him and said without pause or preamble: "Lyndon, I know we can expect a fair shake from you, but I also know you are a damn hard man in a fight and that you don't often holler for the referee to intervene. Now, I know, too, that you can get around dear old So and So [a fellow member of the Republican hierarchy] and you can very often persuade dear old Such and Such [another member of the Republican hierarchy] before he really knows what's going on. But I just want to tell you, in case you don't know it, that in me you have got a different breed of cat. You won't persuade me unless I want to be persuaded. And that is that."

Johnson sat silent a moment, contemplating the suddenness and vigor of the onslaught. Then he rose from his chair, walked around the table, shook Bridges' hand and said: "Fair enough, Styles. We know where we stand." Thereafter, he could never really dislike Bridges, deplore him and his views though he often did. They exchanged many a saturnine glance in the Senate years that followed; they fought many a bitter fight with no excessive care for genteel rules of combat. But they finished as friends; wary friends always, rueful friends sometimes, but friends all the same to the end. Johnson would never tolerate behind-the-back slurs upon Bridges; Bridges reciprocated.

Something of this relationship grew up quickly between Johnson and some of the foreign leaders upon whom he called as Vice-President. When, in May of 1961, he went to the Orient to explore the running sore of free world security in South Viet Nam and the endless difficulties of the Southeast Asia Treaty Organization, he confronted some personalities as powerful and demanding as his own.

His report to President Kennedy of that mission showed all this, as it showed also a perceptive awareness of what was happening and what might happen in Southeast Asia. Parts of that report follow here:

MEMORANDUM

TO: The President
FROM: The Vice-President
RE: Mission to Southeast Asia, India and Pakistan

May 23, 1961

The mission undertaken May 9, 1961, at your request, was informative and illuminating far beyond my expectations. Unusual candor—as well as unusual length—marked exchanges in each country. The purpose of this brief memorandum is to convey concisely such of my own impressions and evaluations as seem most pertinent to decisions now under your consideration. It would be wholly unrealistic to assume that such valid visits afford any basis for substantive policy judgments. It would be equally unrealistic not to recognize that the circumstances and timing of this mission elicited a depth and substance of expression not normally present in exchanges through usual channels. My purpose is to offer perspective—not, I wish to emphasize, to propose policy.

Beyond question, your judgment about the timing of our mission was correct. Each leader—except Nehru—publicly congratulated you on the "timing" of this mission. Chiang said—and all others privately concurred—that the mission had the effect of "stabilizing" the situation in the Southeast Asian nations.

Our mission arrested the decline of confidence in the United States. It did not—in my judgment—restore any confidence already lost. The leaders were as explicit and courteous as courtly men could be in making it clear that deeds must follow words—soon.

We didn't buy time—we were given it.

If these men I saw at your request were bankers, I would know—without bothering to ask—that there would be no further extension on my note.

Starting with President Diem at Saigon, it was my conclusion that the interests of the United States would be served —and protected—by the issuance of joint communiqués. My purpose was this: To attach the signature and the name of each of the leaders to a joint public statement embodying acceptance of each and agreement with the details of your letters which I delivered in your behalf. Without such statements in writing, it was clear that the United States could be victimized later by self-serving statements that you—and the Administration—had offered "nothing" or "too little," etc.

As you recognized, the joint communiqués followed item by item the statements in your letters. In most instances, where substantive pledges and policies were involved, the communiqués were cleared through Washington before issuance. The extensive, important and almost unprecedented communiqué with Nehru largely reflects the high regard the Indian Government holds for Ambassador Galbraith.

I should make these two points clear: Assurances I gave were those you sent me to convey, and no commitments were asked and none were given beyond those authorized in your letters. In some instances, for various reasons, I did not express all the commitments or proposals authorized in the State position papers.

I cannot stress too strongly the extreme importance of following up this mission with other measures, other actions, and other efforts. . . .

I have reached certain other conclusions which I believe may be of value as guidance for those responsible in formulating policies.

These conclusions are as follows:

The battle against Communism must be joined in Southeast Asia with strength and determination to achieve success there—or the United States, inevitably, must surrender the Pacific and take up our defenses on our own shores. Asian Communism is compromised and contained by the maintenance of free nations on the subcontinent. Without this inhibitory influence, the island outposts—Philippines, Japan, Taiwan—have no security and the vast Pacific becomes a Red Sea.

The struggle is far from lost in Southeast Asia and it is by no means inevitable that it must be lost. In each country it is possible to build a sound structure capable of withstanding and turning the Communist surge. The will to resist—while now the target of subversive attack—is there. The key to what is done by Asians in defense of Southeast Asian freedom is confidence in the United States.

There is no alternative to United States leadership in

Southeast Asia. Leadership in individual countries—or the regional leadership and cooperation so appealing to Asians—rests on knowledge and faith in United States power, will and understanding.

SEATO is not now and probably never will be the answer because of British and French unwillingness to support decisive action.

We should consider an alliance of all the free nations of the Pacific and Asia who are willing to join forces in defense of their freedom. Such an organization should:

a) Have a clear-cut command authority.
b) Should also devote attention to measures and programs of social justice, housing, land reform, etc.

Any help—economic as well as military—we give less developed nations to secure and maintain their freedom must be a mutual effort. These nations cannot be saved by United States help alone. To the extent the Southeast Asian nations are prepared to take the necessary measures to make our aid effective, we can be—and must be—unstinting in our assistance. It would be useful to enunciate more clearly than we have—for the guidance of these young and unsophisticated nations— what we expect or require of them.

In large measure, the greatest danger Southeast Asia offers to nations like the United States is not the momentary threat of Communism itself. Rather, that danger stems from hunger, ignorance, poverty and disease. We must—whatever strategies we evolve—keep these enemies at the point of our attack, and make imaginative use of our scientific and technological capability in such enterprises.

The basic decision in Southeast Asia is here. We must decide whether to help these countries to the best of our ability or throw in the towel in the area and pull back our defenses to San Francisco and a "Fortress America" concept. More important, we would say to the world in this case that we don't live up to treaties and don't stand by our friends. This is not my concept. I recommend that we move forward promptly with a major effort to help these countries defend themselves. I consider the key here is to get our best people to control, plan, direct and exact results from our military aid program. In Vietnam and Thailand, we must move forward together.

In Vietnam, Diem is a complex figure beset by many problems. He has admirable qualities, but he is remote from the people, is surrounded by persons less admirable and capable than he. The country can be saved—if we move quickly and wisely. We must have coordination of purpose in our country team, diplomatic and military. The most important thing is imaginative, creative American management of our military aid program.

The Republic of China on Taiwan was a pleasant surprise to me. I had long been aware of the criticisms against Chiang Kai-shek and his government and cognizant of the deep emotional American feelings in some quarters against him. I know these feelings influence our U S policy. Whatever the cause, a progressive attitude is emerging there. Our conversations with Chiang and Mme. Chiang were dominated by discussions of measures of social progress, to my gratified surprise. As with the Republic of Germany in Western Europe, so I believe we might profitably and wisely encourage the Republic of China in Asia to export talents, skills, and resources to other Asian lands to assist in programs of progress.

India could well be the subject of an entire report. Nehru, during our visit, was clearly "neutral" in favor of the West. This Administration is highly regarded and well received in India. Only part of this flows out of hope or expectation of aid. Mainly, there is an intellectual affinity, or an affinity of spirit. This, in my judgment, should be exploited, not with the hope

of drawing India into our sphere—which might be as unneces-
sary as it would be improbable—but, chiefly, with the hope of
cementing under Nehru an India-U S friendship which would
endure beyond any transition of power in India.

President Ayub in Pakistan is singularly impressive. He is
seasoned as a leader where others are not; confident, straight-
forward and, I would judge, dependable. . . . Ayub understands—and is in agreement with—the aims of eradicating
poverty, ignorance and disease. We can have great influence
and achieve dramatic success by supporting Pakistan's needs.
Our military should see how to improve the effectiveness and
achieve modernization of Pakistan's army. Ayub is wisely
aware of Pakistan's strategic position, wants to make his forces
more modern, and wants to resolve the Kashmir dispute to
release Indian and Pakistani troops to deter Chinese rather
than each other. He spells out the fact that U S leadership
rests on our own self-confidence and the confidence we permit
Asians to have in us.

To recapitulate, these are the main impressions I have
brought back from my trip.

The fundamental decision required of the United States—
and time is of the greatest importance—is whether we are to
attempt to meet the challenge of Communist expansion now in
Southeast Asia by a major effort in support of the forces of
freedom in the area or throw in the towel. This decision must
be made in a full realization of the very heavy and continuing
costs involved in terms of money, of effort and of United States
prestige. It must be made with the knowledge that at some
point we may be faced with the further decision of whether we
commit major United States forces to the area or cut our losses
and withdraw should our other efforts fail. We must remain
master of this decision. What we do in Southeast Asia should
be part of a rational program to meet the threat we face in the

region as a whole. It should include a clear-cut pattern of the specific contributions to be expected by each partner according to his ability and resources. I recommend we proceed with a clear-cut and strong program of action.

I believe that the mission—as you conceived it—was a success. I am grateful to the many who labored to make it so.

LYNDON B. JOHNSON

This sort of report and analysis from a Vice-President to a President was probably unique in the relationship it showed between the two offices; in its breadth; in its mixture of hope and skepticism, of eager determination and hard-eyed realism.

Johnson's missions, however, were not all of this sort; sometimes he went not so much to find the facts of some trouble abroad and to make recommendations, as to carry a message of the Kennedy administration's resolve to stand at all costs by our allies. Thus, his best known speech as President Kennedy's emissary was delivered in Berlin on August 19, 1961, when the Soviet Union and the East German Communists had created what had seemed, up to that time, to be the most serious crisis since the Berlin blockade of Truman's days as President.

"I have come to Berlin," Johnson said, "by direction of President Kennedy."

He wants you to know—and I want you to know—that the pledge he has given to the freedom of West Berlin and to the right of Western access to Berlin is firm. To the survival and to the creative future of this city we Americans have pledged, in effect, what our ancestors pledged in forming the United States: "Our lives, our fortunes, and our sacred honor."

I come here at a moment of tension and danger—in your lives, the lives of my countrymen, and the common life of the Free World.

A barrier of barbed wire has been thrown across your city. It has broken for you—and more important, for your brethren to the East—vital human and communal ties—ties that reach back into the lives of families and friends and into the long life of this great city.

I understand the pain and outrage you feel.

I understand the anger you feel as the Communist authorities and their hirelings congratulate themselves on having throttled the flow of men, women and children who could stand it no longer and have come to the West, even at the cost of abandoning their homes, the familiar places, and all they had created.

What a victory they claim! What a failure they prove!

I tell you the Communists congratulate themselves too soon.

Stop for a moment and consider what this crisis is about.

This crisis has arisen because of a massive fact of history. The free men of Germany—both here and in West Germany —have succeeded in these years since the end of the war beyond our more optimistic hopes. I am not referring only to their economic success which all the world knows and admires. They succeeded in far more important ways. They have built a vital democratic life. They have accepted with admirable self-discipline restraints on their military establishment. They have played a great constructive role in making a United Europe. They are now coming to play a major role on the world scene—from India to Bolivia.

Meanwhile, in East Germany there has been a terrible and tragic failure. Despite every instrument of force and propaganda, despite every asset of German skill and German resources, the Communists have not been able to create a life to which men can commit their talents, their faith, and the future of their children.

Make no mistake. This fact of history is well understood in the Kremlin. What they are trying to do now is to interpose barbed wire, bayonets, and tanks against the forces of history.

In the short run, the barbed wire is there; and it will not go away by a wave of the hand. But in the long run this unwise effort will fail. Lift your eyes from these barriers and ask yourselves who can really believe that history will deny Germany and Berlin their natural unity; who can really believe that the German people will choose Communism after what they have seen on German soil.

This is a time, then, for confidence, for poise, and for faith —for faith in yourselves.

It is also a time for faith in your allies, everywhere throughout the world. This island does not stand alone. You are a vital part of the whole community of free men. Your lives are linked not merely to those in Hamburg, Bonn and Frankfurt. They are also linked with those who live in every town of Western Europe, Canada and the United States, and with those on every continent who live in freedom and are prepared to fight for it.

I repeat; this is a time for confidence, for poise, and for faith—qualities with which you have associated the name of your city—from one end of the world to the other—since 1945.

What President Kennedy said on July 25th to his fellow countrymen I now say to you: "With your help and the help of other free men, this crisis can be surmounted. Freedom can prevail—and peace can endure."

14

THE JOHNSON "STYLE"

TO LYNDON JOHNSON THE PRESIDENCY is a challenge, a hope, a burden, and, frankly, a joy. Given his capacity and temperament, he now has an historic opportunity to fulfill the high and lonely task for which he has so long been preparing himself. He is first of all President of the United States, but he is also the active head of a political party; the tireless prodder of a Congress; and the leader of an often recalcitrant Western Alliance.

He also, of course, has a private life—both as the head of a family and as a man with much zest for life. He is an excellent horseman, an expert rifle shot, and a compulsive competitor in everything he attempts. Soon after his move to the White House, the new President spent a weekend at the presidential retreat in Maryland originally called Shangri-la by Franklin Roosevelt and renamed Camp David by Dwight Eisenhower after his grandson. The President's restless energy took him to a bowling alley in one of the lodge's many outbuildings. He had never before found time for this game, but he eyed the alley with great and immediate interest and having carefully watched his guests through a frame or two, moved to the firing line, hurling a staccato string of questions as he did so. He flung the ball with great speed down the alley. The throw was overdone and went a bit to the right. Still, on this first try he downed seven pins and a friend congratulated him. "Pretty good for the first time." Johnson, however, had already gathered that the purpose of the game was to knock down all ten pins with *one* ball. Clearly dissatisfied with his performance, he readjusted his stance, put a bit more control on his arm and sighted down the alley like a man pointing a deer gun. This time he did the job. All ten pins went down and the attendant called out: "A strike, Mr. President!"

Thereafter, he was never satisfied with any throw that did not produce a strike, though he would accept a spare with only minor dissatisfaction. Camp David, in this, his first visit, was put on notice that this President required vast outlet for his energies. When he is not bowling, he is walking about the place with long strides, more or less dragging forward those who accompany him. He works far too much and far too long, and though Mrs. Johnson and all others close to him are ceaselessly at him to let up a bit, there is never a hope that he will do so.

When he returned to the Senate in late 1955 after his heart attack, with many protestations that he had at last learned that one must sometimes relax, it took only two weeks until he was back at his old pace. One afternoon Johnson's personal physician from Texas was a visitor in his office. A mutual friend took the doctor aside and said: "Lyndon is going full tilt at his work again; can't you make him take it a little easier?" The doctor smiled. "In nine hundred and ninety-nine cases out of a thousand," he said, "that would be the right prescription. But in this one case the fundamental human material is different. Unmedical as it may sound to you, the fact is that for Lyndon work and challenge and struggle are the vital forces of life. All this is good, not bad, for him."

However, it may seem to others, the Johnson "style" in the White House is surely based upon the President's own belief that life is not made for the sluggard or the timid. Not only does he often work a sixteen-hour day; he also often leaves the White House for impromptu calls on friends—possibly official friends at the Capitol, possibly quite unofficial ones around Washington. And he and Mrs. Johnson have more friends of both kinds than any other presidential couple in recent history. Male friends the President will sometimes greet in the White House swimming pool. There, slowly paddling about with his eyeglasses still on, he will discuss the events of the day with his guest, on the theory that there is no harm in mixing a little business with his sport. Leaving the swimming pool to go back to the White House proper, he may make a few small detours, to check some matter with a member of his staff, to call an acquaintance on the telephone, or simply to pass a moment or two with a White House guard. Recently, as a young man was looking over photographs of the President in the White House press office, he casually looked around on hearing a footstep entering the room. Not being an habitué of the White House and not knowing Lyndon Johnson, the young man froze on seeing that it was the President who had strolled in. After an introduction and a few casual remarks, the President left, saying in a drawl, "Well, I've got to go and fret about Cuba."

The tone of the administration is one of enormous activity blended with great informality. Informality was not much in evidence in Eisenhower's time, for in his day, the chief presidential assistant, originally Sherman Adams, pretty well gave the tone, and was markedly zealous for Eisenhower's privacy. Entry to the presidential presence was not easily attained even by the most powerful of Republicans. Informality was much in evidence in Kennedy's time, but again there is now a sharp difference. While President Johnson sees more people head-to-head than Kennedy, and is usually more outgoing in manner, when he feels he is officially on duty people do not lightly interrupt him. Generally, he calls them when he needs them; they do not pop in without invitation to exchange the time of day.

Eisenhower was an essentially remote figure, the prototype of the head of state in the European sense. Kennedy, though by no means remote, was essentially shy. One did not find him roaming about Washington with Johnson's persistent restlessness.

Johnson, who seems an extrovert to others but is in truth often an introvert, is both closer and not so close to his staff as was Kennedy. He is closer in the personal and social sense; even Kennedy's alter-ego in his work, Theodore Sorenson, was not often at the White House when in the evening cocktails were being passed. But where Kennedy in his working day treated employees more or less as equals, Johnson treats them more as valued subordinates, but quite clearly subordinates. At work he is in fact a lonelier man, at any point of decision, than was Kennedy. But when the working day is over he is more gregarious with his White House people than was Kennedy.

Eisenhower as President spent most of his social time with men powerful in business and industry. Kennedy saw many writers and artists and persons of Society or Café Society who were amusing companions. Johnson does not foregather with intellectuals to the degree that Kennedy did, although he is not averse to them. First of all, his life has not led him to know well many such men, for it has been spent almost exclusively in public affairs. And second, he cannot quite bring himself to contemplate a whole evening in which the subject of politics, domestic or international, is either wholly absent or is spoken of by men and women to whom it is a pretty dull and recondite subject.

Thus, the tone of the Johnson White House is, in a way, more complicated than it was under either Eisenhower or Kennedy, who were both somewhat less complex than the man who has succeeded them. Johnson's sweeping personal and social gestures—dashing out of the White House to pop in at some surprised friend's luncheon table in Washington, or dancing old-fashioned steps with a kind of gusty decorum at formal White House receptions—have led some to say that his is the "breezy" Administration. It is an over-simplification, as is the collateral notion that he has simply moved the wide social gestures of Texas to 1600 Pennsylvania Avenue, complete with everything save barbecues on the lawn. If there is breeziness, there are also occasional gestures which are unexpectedly punctilious.

Not long after his accession to the Presidency, Johnson

pained and astounded the White House servants by going about at night turning off all lights not absolutely necessary for getting around the place. This was while he was performing his first budget-cutting enterprise, and the common assumption was that once all this had passed the lights would go on again. The President, it was supposed, was only making a small bit of propaganda for extreme frugality. All the same the lights stayed off after the budget crisis had passed; the President simply thought the old mansion need not be lit up all through the night from basement to roof. He so advised Mrs. Johnson and all White House functionaries; if they smiled, he did not see them at it.

Under him, the administration is most carefully organized, and a crispness in operation and terseness in speech are demanded from all hands. The State Department, which even more than the Pentagon is notorious in Washington for using a bureaucratic patois of almost unbreakable code, was early put on notice that the President wanted its papers greatly cut down and, as the directive went, "written in the English language." This was not simply because Johnson has far too much to read every day and night, it was more truly because he believes that government jargon is often used by presidential advisers, consciously or sub-consciously, to avoid taking a clear position or in excessive timidity, a quality which in associates annoys him far more than excessive belligerence.

Cabinet officers are given both more hearing and more responsibility than in the Kennedy days and are firmly held to the letter of those responsibilities. A high official holding primary responsibility for a peculiarly delicate foreign problem told the President orally at some length of his difficulties, seeking a lead from the top as to what course he should take. "Who is in charge of this problem you are talking about?" Johnson asked, looking up briefly from the work on his desk and then bending his head to it again in dismissal. The official blushed, said, "I am, Mr. President," and departed. He had been pinked; but on reflection he did not mind. Johnson had not merely rebuked him; he had also told him that as long as he stayed in his job he had instant and unquestioning backing from the top.

Kennedy, whose general tolerance was high, had one special hostility and that was to what he called "whiners" in his administration. Johnson, too, dislikes "whiners," but even more he detests pretentiousness in staff advice and mere random observations calculated not so much to illuminate a problem as to indicate the wide, eager reading habits of the speaker. "Yes, yes," he may say, "I know about the philosophic implications of the population explosion in the world and all that, and how tough everything is in general. But you came in here—didn't you?—to tell me what you think about such and such a matter on which we really can't wait to act until all these other questions are settled."

Kennedy's administration was not only essentially urban-based in its constituency but to a great degree also eastern urban-based. Before Johnson became President, tests of his personal popularity had indicated that his own homeland, in the political sense, was more clearly the Midwest, the Far West and the South. Within a few months, however, those current oracles of American public affairs, the polls, were showing him with a national popularity precisely as high in the East as in the South. Indeed, a Louis Harris poll in mid-February gave him an immense lead in every section over any Republican challenger for the elections of November, 1964.

Johnson's Presidency is in a sense more truly national than that which went before. In a sense, it is also more in an American tradition. Johnson, the supreme non-organization man demanding a highly organized administration beneath him, represents the composite face of the country more nearly than did Kennedy—the West as well as the East, the South as well as the North. Geographically, Kennedy was a minority President; a map of the electoral results of 1960 shows him all but blacked out west of the Mississippi.

Geographically, Johnson is a more continental President. His voice and manner and personal style are part of the American mosaic of voice and manner and style, while Kennedy's voice and manner and style were a mixture of the Ivy League colleges, the Eastern seaboard, and the Irish-American urban political leaders from Boston on the northeast to Chicago on the west.

While it would carry the thing much too far to suggest that Kennedy's was exclusively an administration of city men with or without multiple academic degrees, it is equally far fetched to suggest that Johnson's is an administration of "you-all types"—westerners and mid-westerners at home only on the ranges, the feed lots, or the oil fields. A somewhat precious myth grew up about Kennedy—privately, by the way, to his sardonic amusement and embarrassment—that his tenancy of the White House had brought to national affairs a unique flowering of bright and sensitive young men who were pleased to accept the services, but not the comradeship, of the tough, and ageless Irish-directed political machine which had nominated him and in good part elected him to the Presidency.

This was a nonsensical notion. Kennedy, who was engagingly and thoroughly honest with himself and others, was never happy at the attitude of these people that his administration was really just a matter of We Happy Few. In the presidential campaign of 1960 "The Jumpers" —the squealing, rapturous teenagers who went into ecstacies at his every appearance—annoyed and even revolted him. Just so the aura thrown about him, for all he could do to resist it, of the Young Prince come at last to power in some modern fable of knighthood, drew in private his sour, apologetic grimaces.

Still, there *was* some such aura about him; and only the murderous waste of his assassination prevented this circumstance from becoming a heavy political burden to him in 1964. Practically all the country admired him personally. But a good deal of the country, by every sign, felt that some of those around him were erecting a spurious fence between the Kennedy retinue and the rest of America.

None of this was in the slightest degree Kennedy's fault (indeed from first to last his partisan and ideological enemies were far less harmful to him than his overly affectionate friends). The fact remained, however, that some of his wisest advisers were often seriously troubled by the situation. Gathered about him, moreover, were not only some authentic and profoundly useful intellectuals—men like Arthur Schlesinger, Jr., McGeorge Bundy, Harlan Cleveland, and Theodore Sorenson—but also some merely presumptive egg-heads whose quotient of learning was as dubious as their political notions were lower-grade collegiate. These latter, along with the social climbers who exploited the late President's tolerant friendship as though they were all one jolly fraternity, sometimes cast about the scene an impression of arrested juvenility which was basically quite false and unfair but which was nevertheless basically harmful.

Johnson came to the Presidency in an atmosphere of profound public grief for a good and beloved President. But there was also genuine public hope, however inchoate and confused, that Washington would return to its old role as a truly national seat of national power, rather than what some feared was a regionalized administration wielding a national power well understood by the President but not always by the Happy Few.

He also came to the Presidency bearing some of the burdens that Harry S. Truman had to bear when he succeeded Franklin D. Roosevelt. Kennedy had been for some, although it offended his own great sense of realism, a sentimentalized and idealized reincarnation of Roosevelt—a man he never was and never wanted to be. The fact that Roosevelt came from a family prominent on the eastern seaboard, an area assumed by some to be necessarily very chic, attracted to him some who snobbishly found such a President "suitable," as well as some who hoped that a bit of the social glamor might rub off on them.

When he died, and the outlander Truman came upon the scene, these people were twice bereaved. They rightly and decently mourned a man; but they also foolishly mourned one they believed had given them the opportunity to become members of a national elite. They began to undermine the Truman administration with whispers of "little man" and "that fellow Truman," long before the official opposition, the Republicans, had opened fire upon him; indeed, with a silliness not at any time approached by the Republicans.

Johnson, as Kennedy's successor, was also an outlander to many of the same people. His difficulties were increased, as had been Truman's, simply by reason of being where a much loved predecessor had so lately been. He was an outlander simply because he was not a Kennedy, as Truman had been an outlander simply because he was not a Roosevelt. He was also, of course, outside the "Society" of the eastern seaboard, as Truman had been, although his family had held a respected position in this country for more than two centuries.

However silly, the emotional rejection of Johnson by many of the less adult and secure of the Kennedy following was and is a problem for the new President, since he must hold the Democratic Party together without significant defections. This in part explains Johnson's persistent deference to some of the outward forms of the Kennedy administration. These forms are, to the new President, a gesture to the past, but they are also good politics.

But in many respects, Lyndon Johnson's position is immensely different from that of Truman. In the first place there is the fact, already mentioned, that Johnson's role as

Vice-President was far different from Truman's. He came to the Presidency already a vital figure in national and world politics. Furthermore, while Truman's place on the Democratic ticket in 1944 was of very little political significance, Lyndon Johnson's in 1960 may well have been the factor which decided the result of the election. Finally, Johnson entered the highest office in the nation after a long and powerful career in national government which developed his almost unique talents for politics to a very high degree of competence. Truman, a strong and courageous President, had never been an entirely effective politician after leaving the somewhat parochial arena of Missouri.

As President, even after his surprising election in 1948, Truman never truly controlled the Democratic Party. Johnson's grip upon the party instrumentalities, once he was in the White House, was necessarily tentative at first, but it hardened month by month, as the year 1964 spun out. He walked warily but skillfully between the legitimate if somewhat nostalgic claims of the Kennedy appointees who dominated the Democratic National Committee and other positions of political power, and the necessity slowly to alter those mechanisms to his own needs and purposes.

This has been done not only in natural pursuit of his own fortunes in the campaign for re-election in November of 1964. Johnson has been motivated also by the fact that he is the most national-minded President since Roosevelt, whom he resembles as a political leader more than Kennedy ever did.

Roosevelt was a profoundly intuitive President, both

as the leader of the country and as the head of his party. The total impact of the celebrated Brain Trust upon him was no more than the impact of a skilled mechanic on a racing-car driver. Mechanics are useful, but they do not operate the machine. So with Johnson and his advisers; they propose but he disposes, to a degree that was never true in Kennedy's relationship with those about him. Roosevelt, unlike Truman, thought consistently of the Democratic Party not as a traditional and all-sufficient body, but as a central weapon to which, given determination and luck, he would add other weapons seized from friendly political independents and unwary Republicans. Incessantly, he was trying to expand his base of power beyond his party; and most of the time this was precisely what he did. So, to, with Johnson.

Roosevelt never had a sectional thought; East, West, North, South were all one to him so long as they went for Roosevelt in the critical autumns of his time. So, too, again, with Johnson. His drive is never merely to win, but to win with so unarguable a majority as to be able to say in complete confidence that he represents not a decisive congeries of *some* national areas, but a totality of the nation. The loss of the West was no pleasant experience to Kennedy; all the same, it was not in his mind a shattering thing. To Johnson the loss of any section would be a dreadful personal blow. For the ideal of one nation is perhaps the strongest force in his political life. As a boy of twenty he was writing earnestly if not gracefully, as editor of the campus paper in the State Teachers College, of the inevitability—and propriety—of the death of sectionalism in American public life. This youthful editorial expressed what has remained his ultimate purpose as a politician.

Again, Roosevelt was alternately very careful and almost excessively bold. In Johnson, too, there is this odd metronomic effect of violent sortie followed by prudent reticence. As a new President he opened a more risky and more trustful series of probes toward possible accommodations with the Russians than Kennedy had been prepared to chance. And as a new President he early showed both more sympathy for the residual colonial problems of old western allies and less tolerance for the tendencies of those allies to strike out on their own in cold war policy.

Though no man can say for certain, it is extremely likely that Kennedy would have been more patient and forebearing with continued allied trade with Castro Cuba in the early part of 1964 than Johnson was willing to be. Unable to persuade old friends, notably Britain, to halt these shipments, he took the bold step of curtailing American military aid to countries deemed the worst offenders.

The amount of aid involved, to be sure, was nominal; the action, however, had great symbolic significance. It meant that Johnson, whose background as an internationalist is long and unqualified, was serving notice that he would not tolerate, for both domestic and foreign reasons, persistent allied acts against vital American interests. Kennedy, one believes, would have finessed the issue, in the hope that a more reasonable allied attitude would at length prevail. Johnson felt the time had come to assert beyond the possibility of further doubt the proposition that the United States was not merely the ostensible but also the actual leader in all affairs touching the Western Hemisphere, *and intended so to remain.*

But where Kennedy committed himself with little reservation to a vast and, to some minds, a quite unattainable reform and rehabilitation of the whole of Latin America in the Alliance for Progress, Johnson approached the matter with some of the reserve of a country banker and all the skepticism of a politician unwilling to put a foot forward until he had tested and retested every inch of the terrain. Like Roosevelt, he chooses his own risks; like Roosevelt, he is at times not subject to restraint and at other times too restrained and cautious for the taste of those about him.

Truman had a marked touch of regionalism in his makeup. Though he apprehended the wide world so well as to be perhaps the most creative American leader of all in foreign policy, he never really knew this country outside his native Southwest and the nearby Middle West. Johnson, again like Roosevelt, not only knows it all; but to him, at bottom, *it is all the same.* Only Eisenhower, in the years since Roosevelt, approached Johnson's tactile awareness of every region, and his deep, compulsive need to speak for the whole country. And even Eisenhower, because his whole career had been spent in the curious half-isolation of professional military life, lacked Johnson's intimate grasp of the various regions in their political aspects.

Here, then, in summary is Lyndon Baines Johnson, the thirty-sixth President of the United States and the fourth President to serve since the close of the Second World

War and the onset of both the atomic age and the Cold War. He is a child of the Great Depression, a partial creator and a full participant in the turn of this country away from the old, nearly total economic individualism toward the responsible social discipline which broke that depression and began the long, still accelerating process of homogenization into a grayer but stronger American society. Few of our Johnson Cities are islands apart any more—economically, socially, politically—and fewer still will be when Lyndon Johnson's administration has run its course.

Having learned in the Second World War the uses and limitations of ultimate force in human affairs, Johnson reached office to confront overmastering challenges to professional political skill. He is one of the most talented politicians in our history, alternately confident and skeptical, outgoing and reserved, tough and compassionate, born to action but sometimes electing to pause in long thought. Can such a man attain three enormously difficult goals: First, an end to political sectionalism in the United States; second, a final accommodation of a race issue that is the greatest domestic problem in a nation now insulated from the shocks of economic disaster; and third, the beginning, at least, of a Western victory in the Cold War, or else a resolution of that war on terms more bearable for the free world?

This will be the test of Lyndon Baines Johnson.

INDEX

INDEX